Nārāyaṇa-Smṛtiḥ

Nārāyaṇa-Smṛtiḥ

नारायणस्मृतिः

composed by
Swami Atmananda

as Guided by
Narayana Guru

Translation by
Swami Muni Narayana Prasad

DK PRINTWORLD
Publishers of Indian Traditions

Cataloging in Publication Data — DK
[Courtesy: D.K. Agencies (P) Ltd. <docinfo@dkagencies.com>]

Atmananda, Swami.
[Nārāyaṇsmṛtiḥ. English & Sanskrit]
Nārāyaṇa-smṛtiḥ = Nārāyaṇsmṛtiḥ / by Swami Atmananda ; translation by Swami Muni Narayana Prasad.
p. cm.
In Sanskrit (Devanagari and roman); translation and pref. in English.
Verse work on Narayana Guru, 1856-1928, Hindu religious leader and social reformer from Kerala.
ISBN: 9788124603925

1. Narayana Guru, 1856-1928. — Poetry. 2. Epic poetry, Sanskrit. 3. Epic poetry, Sanskrit — Translations into English. I. Narayana Prasad, Muni, 1938- II. Title.

DDC 891.21 22

ISBN: 978-81-246-0392-5
First published in India in 2007
Second impression 2015

Printed and published by:
D.K. Printworld (P) Ltd.
Regd. office : *Vedaśrī*, F-395, Sudarshan Park
Ramesh Nagar Metro Station
New Delhi – 110 015
Phones : (011) 2545 3975; 2546 6019; *Fax* : (011) 2546 5926
E-mail: indology@dkprintworld.com
Web: www.dkprintworld.com

Preface

THE source-books of Indian spirituality could generally be classified as *śrutis* and *smṛtis*. *Śruti* means "that which is heard." *Śrutis* contain words uttered by the great *ṛṣis* or seers of the past expounding the ultimate secret they visualized about the meaning and content of our life, and of the world as a whole. In other words, *śrutis* correlate three basic realities: my existence, the existence of the world I perceive, and the one ultimate Reality underlying both. The best examples of this type of spiritual literature are the Upaniṣads. The Vedas are also generally counted as *śrutis*. The reality revealed in such scriptures are of eternal value, meaningful everywhere at any time. The philosophical works of Narayana Guru, like *Ātmopadeśa Śatakam* (One Hundred Verses of Self-Instruction) *Darśanamālā* (Garland of Visions) and the like are of this order.

The word *smṛti* means "that which is remembered." Man is supposed to live in this world of practical affairs by constantly recalling the eternal truths taught in the *śrutis*; only then does life become meaningful. A life lived thus naturally follows certain well-set behaviour patterns. Certain actions would be taboos, and certain others would be enjoined. The former type of directives is known as *niṣedha* (prohibitions), and the latter *vidhi* (directives). The instructional texts written by those who have realized the Reality, giving details of both these kinds of practices, are known as *smṛtis*.

Even as the eternal truth remains one and immutable, necessary adjustments to fit in with time and clime have to be made in the rules of behaviour we formulate with that truth for their firm basis. *Smṛtis*, in other words, are the scriptures that give detailed instructions on prohibitions and directives in life, which necessarily have to make provision for the exigencies of changing temporal and spatial conditions. Such scriptures are known also as Dharmaśāstras (scriptures on righteousness). *Manu-Smṛti* is well known among such. *Yājñavalkya-Smṛti, Parāśara-Smṛti* and *Nārada-Smṛti* are other similar ancient Dharmaśāstras. Purāṇas (mythological legends) and Itihāsas (epics) are also classed under *smṛtis*, for the reason that these texts give emphasis to moral lessons by way of telling stories, rather than to wisdom teaching proper, though references to such could be found in these.

One well-acquainted with the wisdom teaching of *śrutis* need no practical instructions to guide one's life. Such a one's life naturally follows the right path in line with the ultimate truth he knows. *Smṛtis*, thus, are scriptures meant for those who are not familiar with the depth of the wisdom-teachings of *śrutis*. The latter thus being virtually inclusive of the former, the seers who formulate scriptures of the *śruti*-type do not usually compose scriptures of the *smṛti*-type. Perhaps Vyāsa is the one exception to this rule. In fact, Vyāsa is not counted as the name of a particular person, but of a long line of masters or rather editors who composed or edited scriptures both of the *śruti* and *smṛti* types.

All the works of Narayana Guru, even including the hymns, are of the *śruti*-type. Still it is well known how much he was interested is seeing his wisdom reflected in the day-to-day life of humanity, in its individual and social dimensions. Those who are not adepts in scriptural wisdom also have to lead a morally sound life, which requires guidance from authentic persons. The present work, *Nārāyaṇa-Smṛtiḥ*, was written with this end in view.

The Guru, in conformity with customs, did not write it himself. Instead he asked his disciple Swami Atmananda to write it, while offering all the required ideas and guidelines. What the disciple has conveyed through this book in his language contains the ideas and ideals conveyed to him by the Guru. Swami Atmananda himself writes about the origination of this book thus:

> This book contains the teachings imparted by Sri Narayana Guru at Śivagirī Mutt in the month of *Cingam* (August-September) of the Year 1100 ME (AD 1924). The Guru entrusted me with the task of versifying these *dharma*-teachings. What I wrote down each day was read out to the Guru daily, followed by his suggesting necessary corrections. The book thus was completed in a month's time.
>
> *Smṛtis* define *dharma* as follows:
>
> Proper activities suitable to the exigencies of time and clime are called *dharma*.
>
> देशकालोचितं कर्म धर्म ज्ञात्यभिधीयते।
> *deśakālocitaṁ karma dharma jñātyabhidhīyate* ।
>
> Accodingly, the behaviour patterns and belief patterns of people undergo change in accordance with the needs of time and clime. Even when differing in respect of clothing styles and language spoken, humans (at a particular time and clime) have to have something common in respect of customary behaviours and well-established views of life.
>
> The ideas dealt with in the present work are in conformity with such a requirement. Intent on doing away with extravagances and unreasonable pomps, the Guru, the knower of the past, present and future, had brought into

> practice new social customs in conformity with the requirements of the time, as early as thirty-nine years ago. Many of those ideals find place in the present work. Each one adhering to these instructions strictly, will render any other means unnecessary for the actualization of unity of religions and belief patterns, for the well-being of the world and also for world-peace.

This work is named *Nārāyaṇa-Smṛtiḥ* because it conforms to the style of ancient *smṛti*-texts like *Manu-Smṛtiḥ* and *Yājñavalkya-Smṛtiḥ*.

The ancient texts like *Manu-Smṛtiḥ* were written long long ago when temporal, spatial and social conditions were much different from what we have now. Many of the prohibitions and commands given in such texts are apparently outdated now. Many do therefore find fault with such texts altogether. Mere finding fault with an old law or system does no good. What we need is clear-cut guidance acceptable and suitable to the modern times. In other words, we need a new *smṛti*-text befitting the new age. The lacuna that remained thus unfilled was filled by Narayana Guru with one of his disciples as the instrument.

This text definitely will serve as a dependable guide to everyone who intends to live basing his life, both individual and social, on the one ultimate Reality. Those who follow its directives will certainly feel the Guru himself having come before them as a reliable guide.

Though originally written in Sanskrit, it so far has been available in print in the Malayalam script only; nor was any translation or commentary on it available in any other language. This is the first time the *Nārāyaṇa-Smṛtiḥ* comes out with an English translation so that those who are outside Kerala may also have the benefit of it.

Contents

प्रथमः सर्गः (Canto One)

उपोद्घातम्
Introduction

अद्वैतानन्दचिन्मात्रज्योतिर्नारायणात्मकम् ।
चकास्तु धर्मबोधाय नित्यमव्याहतात्मनाम् ॥१॥

advaitānanda-cinmātra-jyotir-nārāyaṇātmakam ।
cakāstu dharmabodhāya nityam avyāhatātmanām ॥1॥

The one effulgence, pure Consciousness and non-dual Happiness in essence, that has assumed the apparent form of Narayana — may It ever remain bright for the sake of teaching righteousness (*dharma*) to those who have clarity of mind. [1]

पावने सह्यपादेऽत्र केरले धर्मराजिते ।
प्राक्कण्वमुनिशार्दूलतपोदीप्त्या विराजितः ॥२॥

pāvane sahyapāde 'tra kerale dharmarājite ।
prāk kaṇvamuniśārdūla tapodīptyā virājitaḥ ॥2॥

At the foot of the holy Sahya ranges, is the region known as Kerala, eminent for the upkeep of righteousness (*dharma*), that remains brightened within by the lustre of the austere self-discipline (*tapas*) practised by the great muni Kaṇva of yore. [2]

श्रीमज्जनार्दनक्षेत्रप्रसाधनपरिष्कृतः ।
केराम्रपनसाशोककदलीपूकसंकुलः ॥३॥

śrīmajjanārdanakṣetraprasādhanapariṣkṛtaḥ ।
kerāmrapanasāśokakadalīpūkasaṅkulaḥ ॥3॥

Adorned with the prosperous Janārdana Temple for cloths, and with the thickly growing coconut and a aracanut palms, mango, jackfruit, aśoka and plantain trees, and the like, [3]

परस्पराश्लिष्टपर्णैर्वारितार्कमरीचिभिः ।
जम्बूद्रुमैश्चोपकूलं नीलया कुल्यया तथा ॥४ ॥

parasparāśliṣṭaparṇair vāritārkamarīcibhiḥ ।
jambūdrumaiścopakūlaṁ nīlayā kulyayā tathā ॥4 ॥

Including jambu trees with their leaves knit together, blocking the free flow of sunlight, and beautified by the seemingly dark rivulets, [4]

गमागमार्थं नौकानां अर्हया च सुरंगया ।
नित्यस्यन्दिस्वच्छजलप्रणालीपरिपावितः ॥५ ॥

gamāgamārthaṁ naukānāṁ arhayā ca suraṅgayā ।
nityasyandisvacchajalapraṇālīparipāvitaḥ ॥5 ॥

With a tunnel that facilitates easier traffic of country boats, and sanctified by constantly running piped natural springs, [5]

पारंगाम्रैर्विशालैश्च व्रीहिक्षेत्रैस्समन्ततः ।
सुगन्धिभिश्च पुन्नागैर्मालक्षेत्रैश्च रञ्जितः ॥६ ॥

pāraṅgāmrairviśālaiśca vrīhikṣetraissamantataḥ ।
sugandhibhiśca punnāgair mālakṣetraiś ca rañjitaḥ ॥6 ॥

Surrounded by cashew groves and extensive paddy fields along with fragrant *punnāga* trees, and beautified by hilly areas, [6]

नाना सस्यसमाकीर्णो देशो वल्कल संज्ञितः ।
अस्त्यस्य नीवृतो रत्नमकुटाकारभासुरः ॥७ ॥

nānā sasyasamākīrṇo deṣo valkala saṁjñitaḥ ।
astyasya nīvṛto ratnamakuṭākāra bhāsuraḥ ॥7 ॥

With thickly growing wild plant-life, is the place named Varkala. Beautifying this place like a crowning gem is, [7]

फलवत्पत्रपुष्पाढ्यो लतापुष्पकरंबितः ।
नेत्राञ्चलविलोकेन नित्यं पादोपसेविनाम् ॥८ ॥

phalavat patrapuṣpāḍhyo latāpuṣpakaraṁbitaḥ ।
netrāñcalavilokeṇa nityaṁ pādopasevinām ॥8 ॥

ईप्सितार्थप्रदानेन राजन्त्या शारदांबया ।
भ्राजिष्णुरमृतास्वादस्वच्छतोयप्रवाहतः ॥९ ॥

īpsitārthapradānena rājantyā śāradāṁbayā ।
bhrājiṣṇur amṛtāsvāda svacchatoyapravāhataḥ ॥9 ॥

आधौतपादस्सश्रीको भक्तानन्दप्रवर्धनः ।
विख्यातो धर्मसंस्थाने रम्यः शिवगिरिर्महान् ॥१० ॥

ādhautapādassaśrīko bhaktānandapravardhanaḥ ।
vikhyāto dharmasaṁsthāne ramyaḥ śivagirir mahān ॥10 ॥

The great hillock named Śivagirī flourishing with wild creepers bearing fruits, leaves and flowers, reigned over by the Goddess Śāradā, who, simply with her glance fulfils all the wishes of those who meditate on her feet, and having surroundings cleansed by the crystal-clear elixir-like water that streams forth constantly, which is prosperous, which heightens the blissfulness of the devout, which is charming, and which also is famous for its concern for upholding righteousness (*dharma*). [8-10]

तत्रैकान्ते सुखासीनश्चूतच्छायोपरञ्जिते ।
आश्रमे धर्ममर्मज्ञो नीतिवैज्ञानिको विभुः ॥११ ॥

tatraikānte sukhāsīnaś cūtacchāyoparañjite ।
āśrame dharmamarmajño nītivaijñāniko vibhuḥ ॥11 ॥

सर्वतन्त्रस्वतन्त्रश्च ब्रह्मनिर्लीनमानसः ।
लोकक्षेमपरो नित्यं भाति नारायणो गुरुः ॥१२ ॥

sarvatantrasvatantraśca brahmanirlīnamānasaḥ ।
lokakṣemaparo nityaṁ bhāti nārāyaṇo guruḥ ॥12 ॥

There, in complete seclusion, resides happily with lustre, the Guru Narayana, in an *āśrama*, under the shade of a mango grove in complete harmony with it, who is the knower of the secret of righteousness (*dharma*), who is also an authority on matters related to justice, who is in a lordly state, who is already free from all conditioning limitations, who remains mentally absorbed in *Brahman*, who is much concerned with the well-being of the world. [11-12]

तं महान्तमुपागम्य धर्मावेक्षणतत्पराः ।
बोधानन्दमुखाश्शिष्याः प्रणिपत्यान्वयुञ्जत ॥१३ ॥

taṁ mahāntam upāgamya dharmāvekṣaṇatatparāḥ ।
bodhānandamukhāśśiṣyāḥ praṇipatyānvayuñjata ॥13 ॥

Having approached that great one, his disciples headed by Bodhānanda, very inquisitive on matters related to righteousness (*dharma*), made enquiries, after prostrating themselves before him. [13]

द्वितीयः सर्गः (Canto Two)

धर्माधर्मविवेचनम्
Discriminating the Righteous from the Unrighteous

शिष्या ऊचुः

भगवान् सर्वतत्त्वज्ञ जीवलोकदयापर ।
धर्माधर्मौ विविच्याद्य श्रोतुमुत्कण्ठिता वयम् ॥१४ ॥

bhagavān sarvatattvajña jīvalokadayāpara ।
dharmādharmau vivicyādya śrotumutkaṇṭhitā vayam ॥14 ॥

The disciples said:

O Lord, O the knower of all the basic principles, O the one compassionate to the entire world of life, we are anxious to hear from you on how to discriminate between righteousness (*dharma*) and unrighteousness (*adharma*). [14]

शंसन्ति केचित्स्वमतं द्विषन्त्यन्यमतं जनाः ।
द्वेषान्मते विरोधाच्च जातावीशे विकल्पनात् ॥१५ ॥

śaṁsanti kecit svamataṁ dviṣantyanyamataṁ janāḥ ।
dveṣānmate virodhācca jātāvīśe vikalpanāt ॥15 ॥

Some praise their own religion, and there are people who hate the religion of others, owing to religious hatred as well as to confusion about matters related to casteism and God. [15]

केचित् स्पृश्याः परेऽस्पृश्याः केचिद्दूरापसर्पणाः ।
केचित् सन्ति सदाचाराः केचिद्दुश्चरितास्तथा ॥१६ ॥

kecit spṛśyāḥ pare 'spṛśyāḥ kecid dūrāpasarpaṇāḥ ।
kecit santi sadācārāḥ kecid duścaritās tathā ॥16 ॥

Some are touchables, and some others are untouchables. Some are allowed to stand only far away. Some behave properly, and some behave badly. [16]

ऐकमत्यवियुक्ताश्च विवादविहताशयाः ।
परस्परेण स्पर्धन्ते केचिज्जात्यभिमानतः ॥१७ ॥

aikamatyaviyuktāśca vivādavihatāśayāḥ ।
paraspareṇa spardhante kecij jātyabhimānataḥ ॥17 ॥

There are those who proud of belonging to a particular caste, lack unanimity, and there are also those who, having become involved in controversies, have no idea of their own and hate each other. [17]

यथाकामं चरन्त्येके शौचाचारादिवर्जिताः ।
अनेकदेवविश्वासादुन्मत्ता इव सर्वतः ॥१८ ॥

yathākāmaṁ carantyeke śaucācārādivarjitāḥ ।
anekadevaviśvāsād unmattā iva sarvataḥ ॥18 ॥

A few behave as they like, with no regard for proper behaviour patterns. They, believing in many gods, live as if gone mad in all respects. [18]

अहो जातिपिशाचस्य बाधया चित्तविभ्रमात् ।
केचिन्मत्सरिणो भूत्वा हिंसन्त्यन्यानकिञ्चनान् ॥१९ ॥

aho jātipiśācasya bādhayā cittavibhramāt ।
kecin matsariṇo bhūtvā hiṁsanty anyān akiñcanān ॥19 ॥

What a pity! Haunted by the fiend of casteism and thus fully confused in mind, some become competitive and do harm to the indigent. [19]

प्रतिकर्तुमशक्तास्ते जातिशल्यनिकृन्तनम् ।
मतमन्यत्समाश्रित्य सुखं जीवन्ति भारते ॥२० ॥

pratikartum aśaktās te jātiśalyanikṛntanam ।
matam anyat samāśritya sukhaṁ jīvanti bhārate ॥20 ॥

They, wounded by the weopon of casteism and unable to react, take refuge in other religions and live a happy life in India. [20]

श्रुतिस्मृतिपुराणोक्तधर्माचारनिबन्धने ।
विभिन्नमतयः केचिन्नीचां वृत्तिं भजन्ति च ॥२१ ॥

śrutismṛtipurāṇoktadharmācāranibandhane ।
vibhinnamatayaḥ kecin nīcāṁ vṛttiṁ bhajanti ca ॥21 ॥

Some, with regard to adhering to righteousness taught in the Śrutis (basic scriptures), Smṛtis (codes of law) and Purāṇas (mythological legends), resort also to heinous activities. [21]

श्रुतिस्मृत्युदिते कर्मण्यनेके नाधिकारिणः ।
विशिष्टबुद्धिमत्वेऽपि तेषां न्यक्कार ईरितः ॥२२ ॥

śrutismṛtyudite karmaṇy aneke nādhikāriṇaḥ ।
viśiṣṭabuddhimatve 'pi teṣāṁ nyakkāra īritaḥ ॥22 ॥

Many are thought of as not competent to perfom the rites enjoined in the Śrutis and Smṛtis. This belittling occurs even of those who are highly intelligent. [22]

सर्वज्ञस्य जगत्कर्तुस्सर्वशक्तिमतः प्रभोः ।
विभुत्वे रीतिरद्यापि कथमेषोपपद्यते ॥२३ ॥

sarvajñasya jagatkartus sarvaśaktimataḥ prabhoḥ ।
vibhutve rītir adyāpi katham eṣopapadyate ॥२३ ॥

How does this custom become befitting the present age also, when seen in the light of the sovereignty of God, the omniscient, omnipotent and omnipresent Creator of the entire world? [23]

स्थितिमेतां समालोक्य कलुषामनवस्थिताम् ।
व्यामोहमुपगच्छामः सत्यासत्याविवेकतः ॥२४ ॥

sthitim etāṁ samālokya kaluṣām anavasthitām ।
vyāmoham upagacchāmaḥ satyāsatyāvivekataḥ ॥24 ॥

We, perceiving this confusing state of affairs and thus unable to discriminate truth from falsehood, remain utterly puzzled. [24]

सर्वतत्त्वार्थवेत्तासि लोकस्य विविधाकृतेः ।
आपूर्य याच्ञामस्माकं गुरो ह्यनुगृहाण नः ॥२५ ॥

sarvatattvārthavettāsi lokasya vividhākṛteḥ ।
āpūrya yācñām asmākaṁ guro hyanugṛhāṇa naḥ ॥25 ॥

O Guru, the one who knows the basic truth of all that appears variously as this world, kindly bless us by fulfilling this entreaty of ours. [25]

गुरुरुवाचः —

प्रश्नं निशम्य भवतां साधु तुष्यामि वत्सलाः ।
अमुमर्थं चिन्तयतः कालो भूयानगान्मम ॥ २६ ॥

praśnaṁ niśamya bhavatāṁ sādhu tuṣyāmi vatsalāḥ ।
amum arthaṁ cintayataḥ kālo bhūyān agān mama ॥26 ॥

The Guru said:

Dear ones, listening to your questions makes me extremely happy. Most of my time also was being spent on thinking about the very same problem. [26]

धर्म एव हि बोद्धव्यो मन्तव्यः कर्मकोटिषु ।
अनुष्ठेयोपदेष्टव्यो धमो लोकप्रवर्तकः ॥२७ ॥

dharma eva hi boddhavyo mantavyaḥ karmakoṭiṣu ।
anuṣṭheyopadeṣṭavyo dhamo lokapravartakaḥ ॥27 ॥

Dharma (righteousness) is that about which one should become enlightened. *Dharma* is what is to be pondered on, to be practised, and to be taught, in respect of crores (millions) of *karmas* (actions). [27]

अपकर्षकरं किञ्चिदसमञ्जसवर्त्मगम् ।
पुण्यक्षयविधायित्वादाचरेन्न कदाचन ॥२८ ॥

apakarṣakaraṁ kiñcid asamañjasavartmagam ।
puṇyakṣayavidhāyitvād ācaren na kadācana ॥28 ॥

Do not do anything that makes you inferior, and anything that deviates from the right path, for the reason that such actions impair your merits (*puṇya*). [28]

परोपकारनिरतैर्युष्माभिस्सर्वदानघाः ।
अवश्यमनुसन्धेयो धर्मः सर्वार्थसाधकः ॥२९ ॥

paropakāraniratair yuṣmābhis sarvadānaghāḥ ।
avaśyam anusandheyo dharmaḥ sarvārthasādhakaḥ ॥29 ॥

Being constantly interested in doing good to others, you should certainly be seeking for the *dharma*, which is always sinless and is the cause of attaining all that is meaningful in life. [29]

अमुमुद्दिश्य यत्तत्त्वं एतावन्तमनेहसम् ।
व्यचिन्तयं प्रवक्ष्यामि शृणुध्वं तस्य संग्रहम् ॥३० ॥

amum uddiśya yat tattvaṁ etāvantam anehasam ।
vyacintayaṁ pravakṣyāmi śṛṇudhvaṁ tasya saṁgraham ॥30 ॥

I shall tell you in brief the basic principles I have been pondering on till now, with the very same goal in mind. Please listen to me. [30]

यतो धर्मात्मनो दृश्यं आयातं येन जीवति ।
यस्मिन् विलयमाप्नोति तस्मात् सर्वं तदात्मकम् ॥३१ ॥

yato dharmātmano dṛśyaṁ āyātaṁ yena jīvati ।
yasmin vilayam āpnoti tasmāt sarvaṁ tadātmakam ॥31 ॥

The entire visible world emerges from the one Reality that is *dharma* in essence; it lives because of that, and merges back into the very same Reality. For this reason, everything is that Reality in essence. [31]

द्वैविध्यं जगतो भाति चराचरविभागतः ।
चराणां मानवाः श्रेष्ठा विशेषज्ञानयोगतः ॥३२ ॥

dvaividhyaṁ jagato bhāti carācaravibhāgataḥ ।
carāṇāṁ mānavāḥ śreṣṭhā viśeṣajñānayogataḥ ॥32 ॥

Of two kinds are the forms apparent in this world: the movables and the immovables. Amongst the movables, humans are the superiormost because they possess the quality of high thinking. [32]

जातिरेका मनुष्याणां मतमेकमनिन्दितम् ।
देवोप्येकः समासेन जातिरादौ निरूप्यते ॥३३ ॥

jātir ekā manuṣyāṇāṁ matamekam aninditam ।
devopy ekaḥ samāsena jātir ādau nirūpyate ॥33 ॥

Humans are of one *jāti* (kind); their blameless religion or faith is also one alone; and God is also one. First I shall summarily deliberate on *jāti*. [33]

एकजातिविचारम्

(Reflections on Oneness of *jāti*)

अनेकव्यक्तिषु स्यूतं तद्व्यावर्तकलक्षणम् ।
तासु व्यक्तिषु सा जातिर्दोषत्रयविलक्षणा ॥३४ ॥

anekavyaktiṣu syūtaṁ tad vyāvartakalakṣaṇam ।
tāsu vyaktiṣu sā jātir doṣatraya-vilakṣaṇā ॥34 ॥

Those characteristic distinguishing marks that are commonly seen unchanging in a group of individual entities, that enable us to differentiate those groups from other such, constitute *jāti*, free from the three logical defects. [34]

(*Avyāpti* or non-inclusion or exclusion of a part of the thing defined, *ativyāpti* or including what is not intended to be included, and *asambhavam* or impossibility, are the three defects referred to here.)

मनुष्याणां मनुष्यत्वं जातिर्गोत्वं गवां यथा ।
नैव सा ब्राह्मणत्वादिर्यौगिकत्वाद् विमृश्यताम् ॥३५ ॥

manuṣyāṇāṁ manuṣyatvaṁ jātir gotvaṁ gavāṁ yathā ।
naīva sā brāhmaṇatvādir yaugikatvād vimṛśyatām ॥35 ॥

Man's humanity marks out the human kind, even as bovinity proclaims a cow. Brahminhood and the like do not do so. This would be understood when reflected upon, taking all the concerned factors into consideration. [35]

स्त्रीपुंसयोर्मिथो रागाद् ग्राम्यधर्मे यदि प्रजाः ।
जायते जातिरनयोरेकान्या मोहकल्पिता ॥३६ ॥

strīpuṁsayor mitho rāgād grāmyadharme yadi prajāḥ ।
jāyate jātir anayor ekānyā mohakalpitā ॥36 ॥

If male and female, loving each other, mate together and beget offspring, then they are of the same *jāti*; all other ideas (concerning *jāti*) are imaginations of deluded minds. [36]

पृथग्जातिः परिच्छिन्ना व्यक्तीनां मूर्तिराकृतिः ।
स्वरो गन्धो रसः स्पर्शः पृथक् पृथगवेक्ष्यते ॥३७ ॥

pṛthag jātiḥ paricchinnā vyaktīnāṁ mūrtirākṛtiḥ ।
svaro gandho rasaḥ sparśaḥ pṛthak pṛthag avekṣyate ॥37 ॥

It is usually seen that individuals of each *jāti* have a common bodily form, common sound pattern, common smelling habit, common food-taste, and common feeling of touch. [37]

जातिव्यक्तं वपुः स्वस्य जातिं व्यञ्जयति स्वयं ।
चक्षुष्मान् नानुयुञ्जीत का जातिरिति बोधवान् ॥३८ ॥

jātivyaktaṁ vapuḥ svasya jātiṁ vyañjayati svayaṁ ।
cakṣuṣmān nānuyuñjīta kā jātir iti bodhavān ॥38 ॥

An individual entity's body natural to a particular species, reveals clearly, of which *jāti* one is. Those who are well-sighted and intelligent never ask, "To which *jāti* do you belong?" [38]

व्यापारदेशभाषाभिर्या या संज्ञा निगद्यते ।
तां तां वदन्तीह जातिं पामरा न तु पण्डिताः ॥३९ ॥

vyāpāradeśabhāṣābhir yā yā saṁjñā nigadyate ।
tāṁ tāṁ vadantīha jātiṁ pāmarā na tu paṇḍitāḥ ॥39 ॥

Names related to vocation, location, and language are there. Such are often asserted by stupid people as referring to *jāti*. The learned never do so. [39]

ज्ञानवाराशिजन्यानां सर्वेषां वपुषामिह ।
बीजं सामान्यसलिलं मूलं चेत्यभिधीयते ॥४० ॥

jñānavārāśijanyānāṁ sarveṣāṁ vapuṣām iha ।
bījaṁ sāmānyasalilaṁ mūlaṁ cetyabhidhīyate ॥40 ॥

Every individual wave that emerges from the ocean has water alone for its causal substance. Likewise, every apparent form emerging from the ocean of Consciousness has Consciousness alone for causal Reality. This is well known to all. [40]

तन्मनुष्ये मनुष्यत्वं गवि गोत्वं च वानरे ।
वानरत्वं पिके तद्वत् पिकत्वं जातिरुच्यते ॥४१ ॥

tan manuṣye manuṣyatvaṁ gavi gotvaṁ ca vānare ।
vānaratvaṁ pike tadvat pikatvaṁ jātir ucyate ॥41 ॥

Of these, humanity amongst humans, bovinity amongst cows, monkeyhood amongst monkeys, and cuckoohood amongst cuckoos, are said to be their respective *jāti*s. [41]

तस्मात्सर्वमनुष्याणां जातिरेका निरूपिता ।
वेषभाषादेशभेदैर्विकल्पं नानुगच्छति ॥४२ ॥

tasmāt sarvamanuṣyāṇāṁ jātir ekā nirūpitā ।
veṣa bhāṣā deśa bhedair vikalpaṁ nānugacchati ॥42 ॥

Thus it is confirmed that all the humans are of one *jāti*. The differences existing with regard to the way one adorns oneself, language spoken, and the geographical region one inhabits, do not become deciding factors in respect of *jāti*. [42]

अतो जात्यैक्यतो मर्त्याः साहोदर्यविभूतयः ।
सर्वैश्वर्यसमायुक्ता वर्तेरन् वीतमत्सराः ॥४३॥

ato jātyaikyato martyāḥ sāhodaryavibhūtayaḥ I
sarvaiśvaryasamāyuktā varteran vītamatsarāḥ II43 II

Humans, therefore, are to live as the embodiments of fraternity, with no antagonism among them, for the reason that they are of one *jāti*. [43]

एकमतविचारम्
(Reflections on Oneness of Faith)

शिष्या ऊचुः —

भगवन् प्रक्रियां जातेर्निशम्य भवतो मुखात् ।
तृप्ता वयं तदिच्छामः श्रोतुं मतमतः परम् ॥४४॥

bhagavan prakriyāṁ jāter niśamya bhavato mukhāt I
tṛptā vayaṁ tad icchāmaḥ śrotuṁ matam ataḥ param II44 II

The disciples said:

O Lord, we feel fully satisfied on having heard from you the part related to *jāti*. Now we wish to hear about religion (*matam*) from you. [44]

गुरुरुवाच —

मतमेकं मनुष्याणां इति पूर्वमुदीरितम् ।
कीदृक् तदिति संक्षिप्य वक्ष्ये शृणुत साधवः ॥४५॥

matam ekaṁ manuṣyāṇāṁ iti pūrvam udīritam I
kīdṛk tad iti saṁkṣipya vakṣye śṛṇuta sādhavaḥ II45 II

The Guru said:

That all the humans have only one faith or religion (*matam*), I have already stated. I shall now tell you how it is so in a summary fashion; O good ones, listen to me. [45]

अभिप्रायो मतं नाम महतां तत्त्ववेदिनाम् ।
मतस्य सारः सर्वोऽपि वाक्यवैचित्र्यभूषितः ॥४६ ॥

abhiprāyo mataṁ nāma mahatāṁ tattvavedinām ।
matasya sāraḥ sarvo 'pi vākyavaicitryabhūṣitaḥ ॥46 ॥

Matam means the well-conceived opinion of the great ones, the knowers of Reality. Only that the universal content of this *matam* finds verbal expression embellished picturesquely. [46]

अनेकगिरिसंभूता निम्नगेव महोदधिम् ।
एकं सनातनं वस्तुं प्राप्य विश्राम्यति स्वयम् ॥४७ ॥

anekagirisaṁbhūtā nimnageva mahodadhim ।
ekaṁ sanātanaṁ vastuṁ prāpya viśrāmyati svayam ॥47 ॥

Just as various rivers originating from different mountains reach the same ocean and become one with it, (different religions) attain to the one eternal Reality and find repose in it. [47]

तत्तत्कालसमुत्थानादाचार्याणां महात्मनाम् ।
पन्थानो ज्ञानवैचित्र्याद् विचित्रास्सन्ति सर्वतः ॥४८ ॥

tat tat kālasamutthānād ācāryāṇāṁ mahātmanām ।
panthāno jñāna vaicitryād vicitrās santi sarvataḥ ॥48 ॥

For the reason that the great masters emerged at different periods of time, and because their ways of thinking were coloured variously by their expositions of wisdom, religions simply appear to be various everywhere. [48]

तथाऽपि तेषामास्तिक्यं प्राप्यमुद्देश्यमेव च ।
एकतां द्योतयत्येव तदेकं मतमीर्यते ॥४९ ॥

tathā 'pi teṣām āstikyaṁ prāpyam uddeśyam eva ca ।
ekatāṁ dyotayaty eva tad ekaṁ matam īryate ॥49 ॥

In spite of these, they show unanimity in respect of belief in God, the goal to be attained and the purpose of life. That is the one *matam* (opinion) or religion stated here. [49]

माहम्मदाः क्रैस्तवाश्च जैनाबौद्धास्तथेतरे ।
एकतापादनायैव प्रयतन्ते निरन्तरम् ॥५० ॥

māhammadāḥ kraistavāś ca jaināvauddhās tathetare ।
ekatāpādanāyaiva prayatante nirantaram ॥50 ॥

Muslims, Christians, Jainas, Buddhists and others too — all strive constantly to attain oneness alone. [50]

एकत्वमनुसन्धातुं सर्वेषां हि समुद्यमः ।
एकमेव मतं तेषां नात्र पक्षद्वयं मतम् ॥५१ ॥

ekatvam anusandhānaṁ sarveṣāṁ hi samudyamaḥ ।
ekam eva mataṁ teṣāṁ nātra pakṣadvayaṁ matam ॥51 ॥

Everyone's effort is to contemplate on and to attain oneness. All these (religions) are of this same opinion (*matam*). Our opinion is that there is no room for two opinions on this matter. [51]

सामान्यसत्ता सर्वेषां मतानामनुबन्धिनी ।
एकैवातोऽप्येकमेव मतं युक्तिचमत्कृतम् ॥५२ ॥

sāmānyasattā sarveṣāṁ matānām anubandhinī ।
ekaivāto 'pyekam eva mataṁ yukticamatkṛtam ॥52 ॥

The common substance related to all religions is one alone. Therefore, religion, attired with logical reason, is one only. [52]

अनेकमतसिद्धान्तमज्ञात्वैकं हि हस्तिनि ।
अन्धा इव वितण्डोक्तेर्मूढा मुह्यन्ति नेतरे ॥५३ ॥

anekamatasiddhāntam ajñātvaikaṁ hi hastini ।
andhā iva vitaṇḍokter mūḍhā muhyanti netare ॥53 ॥

Unaware of the one final conclusion that various religions arrive at, idiots — not others — get confused with fallacious arguments, like the blind men who perceived an elephant. [53]

मतानि जेतुं शक्यानि न वादेन मिथो बलात् ।
प्रमादेन मतद्वेषी वादमात्रेण नश्यति ॥५४ ॥

matāni jetuṁ śakyāni na vādena mitho balāt ।
pramādena matadveṣī vādamātreṇa naśyati ॥54 ॥

Religions can never be defeated either through arguments or by resorting to force. Religious antagonists, simply motivated by arguments, erroneously destroy themselves. [54]

सर्वे चात्मसुखावाप्त्यै प्रवर्तन्ते प्रवर्तकम् ।
मतमेव सर्वेषां तन्मतमेकं न संशयः ॥५५ ॥

sarve cātmasukhāvāptyai pravartante pravartakam ।
matam eva sarveṣāṁ tan matam ekam na saṁśayaḥ ॥55 ॥

Everyone makes efforts for attaining self-happiness; and this is agreed by all. This opinion (*matam*) is one alone; there is no doubt about it. [55]

एकत्वात् प्रतिपाद्यस्य सर्वं च प्रतिपादकम् ।
मतमेकत्वमेवैति कात्र नानात्वकल्पना ॥५६ ॥

ekatvāt pratipādyasya sarvaṁ ca pratipādakam ।
matam ekatvam evaiti kātra nānātvakalpanā ॥56 ॥

The theme discussed by all religions being one, the doctrines they demonstrate have to aim at one goal alone. How can there be room for the idea of multiplicity in this matter? [56]

निरुक्तजातेरेकत्वान् मतस्यैकत्वमास्थितम् ।
मते नानात्वचिन्ता तु केवलं भान्तिजृंभिता ॥५७ ॥

niruktajāter ekatvān matasyaikatvamāsthitam ।
mate nānātvacintā tu kevalaṁ bhāntijṛṁbhitā ॥57 ॥

The reason that confirms the oneness of *jāti*, that has already been pronounced, establishes the oneness of religion (*matam*) as well. The idea of multiplicity in respect of religions arises simply out of delusion. [57]

"मम वर्त्मानुवर्तन्ते मनुष्याः पार्थ सर्वशः" ।
इति गीतावचोप्यत्र मते प्रामाण्यमर्हति ॥५८ ॥

"mama vartmānuvartante manuṣyāḥ pārtha sarvaśaḥ" ।
iti gītāvacopyatra mate prāmāṇyam arhati ॥58 ॥

"My very path it is, O Pārtha, that all men do tread from every possible approach." These words of the *Bhagavad Gita* also deserve to be considered authoritative in the matter of religions. [58]

एकं वर्त्मानुवर्तन्ते मानवाः सर्वतो मते ।
इत्यबाधान्मतैकत्वं साधितं सर्वसम्मतम् ॥५९ ॥

ekaṁ vartmānuvartante mānavāḥ sarvato mate ।
ity abādhān mataikatvaṁ sādhitaṁ sarvasammatam ॥59 ॥

It always and everywhere remains unchanged that, people, with religions, follow their respective paths aiming at one goal alone. The oneness of religion (*matam*), thus, is acceptable to all. [59]

एकदेवविचारम्
(Reflections on Oneness of God)

शिष्या ऊचुः —

सर्वज्ञास्माकमुच्छिन्नः सन्देहो मतवर्त्मनि ।
एकदेवत्वमप्यस्मात् परं व्याख्यातुमर्हति ॥६० ॥

sarvajñāsmākam ucchinnaḥ sandeho matavartmani ।
ekadevatvam apy asmāt paraṁ vyākhyātum arhati ॥60 ॥

The disciples said:

O the all-knowing one, our religion-related doubts are all destroyed completely. Now the oneness of God also deserves to be elucidated by you. [60]

गुरुरुवाच —

विचित्रस्यास्य जगतः कर्ता विविधशक्तिमान् ।
सर्वेश्वरः स सर्वज्ञ एको देव इतीरितः ॥६१ ॥

vicitrasyāsya jagataḥ kartā vividhaśaktimān ।
sarveśvaraḥ sa sarvajña eko deva itīritaḥ ॥61 ॥

The Guru said:

The Supreme God of manifold potentials, is the creator of this multifarious world. That omniscient one is the one God mentioned here. [61]

तत्त्वान्वेषणनिष्णातैर्विमर्शविशदाशयैः ।
प्रणीता वाक्यपटली सत्तैकस्येति घुष्यति ॥६२ ॥

tattvānveṣaṇaniṣṇātair vimarśaviśadāśayaiḥ ।
praṇītā vākyapaṭalī sattaikasyeti ghuṣyati ॥62 ॥

There are those who are experts in intuitive search for Reality, and who have clear notions arrived at through detailed enquiry. Their authentic words declare that one ultimate Reality alone has existence. [62]

अनेकसत्तोपन्यासे वाक्यार्थस्यानवस्थितिः ।
तदेकः परमो देवो मतवाक्यार्थसम्मतः ॥६३ ॥

anekasattopanyāse vākyārthasyānavasthitiḥ ।
tadekaḥ paramo devo matavākyārthasammataḥ ॥63 ॥

The claim that more than one God exists, results in the fallacy of infinite regression of the connotation of such words. Therefore, one alone is the God that is supreme, and that alone has the approval of scriptural utterances. [63]

विभिन्नमतभाजस्तु सर्वे स्वमतनिश्चितः ।
एको देव इति प्राहुरेकत्वं सर्वसम्मतम् ॥६४ ॥

vibhinnamatabhājastu sarve svamataniścitaḥ ।
eko deva iti prāhur ekatvaṁ sarvasammatam ॥64 ॥

Adherents of different religions, as is well known, clearly state that their concerned religion firmly believes in one God alone. The oneness of God is thus admitted by everyone. [64]

देवे द्वित्वं बहुत्वं वा न कस्यापि मते मतम् ।
जात्यैकत्वं मतैकत्वं दैवैकत्वं तथेष्यते ॥६५ ॥

deve dvitvaṁ bahutvaṁ vā na kasyāpi mate matam ।
jātyaikatvaṁ mataikatvaṁ devaikatvaṁ tatheṣyate ॥65 ॥

No religion admits either duality or multiplicity in respect of God. Such is the way the oneness of *jāti*, oneness of religion and oneness of God are to be understood. [65]

शिष्या ऊचुः —

जातेर्मतस्य देवस्याप्येकत्वं सम्यगीरितम् ।
सामान्यधर्मं मर्त्यानां ब्रूहि धर्मविदां वर ॥६६ ॥

jāter matasya devasyāpyekatvaṁ samyag īritam ।
sāmānyadharmaṁ martyānāṁ brūhi dharmavidāṁ vara ॥66 ॥

The oneness of *jāti*, *matam* and God has been made sufficiently clear. O the greatest amongst the knowers of *dharma* (righteousness), please tell us now about *dharma* in general. [66].

तृतीयः सर्गः (Canto Three)

सामान्यधर्मम्
(Righteousness in General)

गुरुरुवाच —

अहिंसा सत्यमस्तेयः तथैवाव्यभिचारिता ।
मद्यस्य वर्जनं चैवं पञ्चधर्मास्समासतः ॥६७ ॥

ahiṁsā satyam asteyaḥ tathaivāvyabhicāritā ।
madyasya varjanaṁ caivaṁ pañcadharmās samāsataḥ ॥67 ॥

The Guru said:

Not hurting any living being, being truthful, not stealing, giving up liquor, being chaste — these five in short are the five *dharmas*. [67]

अहिंसा परमो धर्मस्सर्वधर्मेषु सुव्रताः ।
बुद्धादयो महात्मानो ययाऽपुः परमं पदम् ॥६८ ॥

ahiṁsā paramo dharmas sarvadharmeṣu suvratāḥ ।
buddhādayo mahātmāno yayā 'puḥ paramaṁ padam ॥68 ॥

Of these, O the ones very strict in adhering to virtues, *ahiṁsā* or not hurting any living being is the most important of all virtues (*dharmas*) to be practised. Great souls like Buddha did attain their supreme goal by adhering to this virtue. [68]

कस्यापि प्राणिनो वत्सा शरीरप्राणचेतसाम् ।
अपीडनमहिंसा स्यान्मनो वाक्कायकर्मभिः ॥६९ ॥

kasyāpi prāṇino vatsā śarīraprāṇacetasām ।
apīḍanam aḥiṁsā syān mano vākkāyakarmabhiḥ ॥69 ॥

O my dear ones, the virtue of not causing hurt to any living being, bodily, mentally or in respect of the vital force (*prāṇa*), through speech, mind or physical action, is known as *ahiṁsā* or not hurting. [69]

धर्माः सर्वेप्यहिंसायां अन्तरंगतया स्थिताः ।
अधर्मा अपि हिंसायां इत्याहुर्धर्मवेदिनः ॥७० ॥

dharmāḥ sarvepy ahiṁsāyāṁ antaraṅgatayā sthitāḥ ।
adharmā api hiṁsāyāṁ ity āhur dharmavedinaḥ ॥70 ॥

All righteousnesses virtually are implicit in the virtue of *ahiṁsā*. So are all unrighteousnesses in *hiṁsā* or the habit of hurting other living beings. Such is the utterance of the knowers of *dharma*. [70]

अहिंसाव्रतशीले तु हिंस्राहिंस्रा हि जन्तवः ।
विश्वासमुपगच्छन्ति मातरीव प्रमोदतः ॥७१ ॥

ahiṁsāvrataśīle tu hiṁsrāhiṁsrā hi jantavaḥ ।
viśvāsam upagacchanti mātarīva pramodataḥ ॥71 ॥

Both fierce and gentle animals happily treat those who practise the virtue of *ahiṁsā*, as trustworthy as their own mothers. [71]

सति साधु भवेत् सत्यं सत्यं ब्रह्म सनातनम् ।
सत्ये तिष्ठति लोकोऽयं वदेत् सत्यं न चानृतम् ॥७२ ॥

sati sādhu bhavet satyaṁ satyaṁ brahma sanātanam ।
satye tiṣṭhati loko 'yaṁ vadet satyaṁ na cānṛtam ॥72 ॥

Of all that has existence, Truth is the best. And *Brahman* is the one eternal Truth. This world has its being in the existence of that Truth. Therefore, tell always truth; never tell lies. [72]

यः सत्यपरवान् नित्यं सत्ये योगीव वर्तते ।
स यद् वक्तीह तत्सर्वं अतर्कितफलावहम् ॥७३ ॥

yaḥ satyaparavān nityaṁ satye yogīva vartate ।
sa yad vaktīha tat sarvaṁ atarkitaphalāvaham ॥73 ॥

The one who relies constantly on truth, who finds himself existing in truth like a yogī — whatever he says doubtlessly becomes fruitful. [73]

परस्वाहृति तच्चिन्ता वर्जिताऽस्तेयसंज्ञिता ।
तदस्तेयप्रतिष्ठायां रत्नोपस्थानमुच्यते ॥७४ ॥

parasvāhṛti tac cintā varjitā 'steyasaṁjñitā ।
tad asteyapratiṣṭhāyāṁ ratnopasthānam ucyate ॥74 ॥

The virtue of avoiding stealing the property of others and even the thought of doing so, is called *asteya* (not stealing). The adage is that, "Becoming well-stabilized in *asteya* means finding oneself in a gemlike presence." [74]

स्तेयस्सर्वापदां हेतुः अस्तेयः सर्वसंपदाम् ।
स्तेयान्मानक्षतिस्तस्मादस्तेयं सर्वदाऽऽचरेत् ॥७५ ॥

steyas sarvāpadāṁ hetuḥ asteyaḥ sarvasaṁpadām ।
steyānmānakṣatis tasmād asteyaṁ sarvadā ''caret ॥75 ॥

Stealing causes all kinds of perils, and not stealing ensures all kinds of prosperity. Stealing results in one's ill-repute. Therefore, always practise the virtue of not stealing. [75]

चौर्यं वर्जयते नित्यं महते करणैस्त्रिभिः ।
विश्वासार्जनता सर्वमुपदीकुरुते स्वयम् ॥७६ ॥

cauryaṁ varjayate nityaṁ mahate karaṇais tribhiḥ ।
viśvāsārjanatā sarvam upadīkurute svayam ॥76 ॥

The entire society on its own trustfully offers everything as gifts before the great one who gives up stealing with the three faculties (mind, speech, and physical action) for ever. [76]

चुराविषसमाक्रान्ति मलीमसनराधमम् ।
निर्भर्त्स्य नूनमस्यन्ति दूरेऽलर्कमिवानघाः ॥७७ ॥

curāviṣa-samākrānti malīmasa-narādhamam ।
nirbhartsya nūnam asyanti dūre 'larkam ivānaghāḥ ॥77 ॥

Sinless ones always censure a heinous and impure man who is poisoned by the habit of stealing, and they keep themselves far away from him. [77]

वीक्षणं परनारीणां कामसंकल्पपूर्वकम् ।
तत्सल्लापाच्च तद्योगो व्यभिचार इति स्मृतः ॥७८ ॥

vīkṣaṇaṁ paranārīṇāṁ kāmasaṁkalpapūrvakam ।
tat sallāpāc ca tadyogo vyabhicāra iti smṛtaḥ ॥78 ॥

Looking lustfully at other's women, having pleasantries with them, and having sexual union with them — these constitute *vyabhicāra* or unchaste behaviour. [78]

स्थानमानधनज्ञानाचाराणां स्वकुलस्य च ।
प्राणस्याकालिको नाशो व्यभिचारेण जायते ॥७९ ॥

sthānamāna-dhana-jñānācārāṇāṁ svakulasya ca ।
prāṇasyākāliko nāśo vyabhicāreṇa jāyate ॥79 ॥

Because of unchaste way of living occur the untimely downfall of one's social status, honour, wealth, knowledge and moral sense as well as of one's own lineage and life. [79]

दिवाप्यन्धं तमः पुंसो व्यभिचारमुपेयुषः ।
तस्मान्नियतिदत्तं यत् सुखं तच्च विनश्यति ॥८० ॥

divāpy andhaṅ tamaḥ puṁso vyabhicāramupeyuṣaḥ ।
tasmān niyatidattaṅ yat sukhaṁ tacca vinaśyati ॥80 ॥

Even day-time appears to be full of darkness to the man who resorts to unchaste life. Nature-given happiness also perishes in his case. [80]

स्वपत्नीपरसंसर्गो कस्यापीह न रोचते ।
वर्जयेद् व्यभिचारं तद् इहामुत्र शुभाग्रही ॥८१ ॥

svapatnī-parasaṁsargo kasyāpīha na rocate ।
varjayed vyabhicāraṁ tad ihāmutra śubhāgrahī ॥81 ॥

No one in this world likes his own wife having sex with others. Therefore, unchaste way of living is to be given up by all those who prefer to be happy here and the hereafter. [81]

बुद्धेर्वैकल्यजनकं मद्यमित्युच्यते बुधैः ।
मद्यसेवां न कुर्वीत मद्यं विषसमं विदुः ॥८२ ॥

buddher vaikalyajanakaṁ madyam ity ucyate budhaiḥ ।
madyasevāṁ na kurvīta madyaṁ viṣasamaṁ viduḥ ॥82 ॥

That which causes disability to intelligence is understood by the knowledgeable as *madya* (liquor). Do not consume liquor. Liquor is thought of as poison-like. [82]

सुरा हि फेनविजयाधूमपत्रादि वत्सलाः ।
चित्तभ्रमविधायित्वान्मद्यत्वेनेह गण्यते ॥८३ ॥

surā hi phenavijayā-dhūmapatrādi vatsalāḥ ।
cittabhramavidhāyitvān madyatveneha gaṇyate ॥83 ॥

Toddy, opium, *gāñjā*, tobacco and the like also, O the dear ones, cause mental derangements. Therefore these also in this context are to be treated as pertaining to the class of liquor (*madya*). [83]

मद्यस्य विक्रयादाने सन्धानं दानमेव च ।
कदापि नाचरेद्धीमान् महापातकहेतुकम् ॥८४ ॥

madyasya vikrayādāne sandhānaṁ dānam eva ca ।
kadāpi nācared dhīmān mahāpātakahetukam ॥84 ॥

Those who are wise should never become involved in buying and selling, stocking and offering of liquors. Doing so causes heinous sin. [84]

मद्यपानाद्वीतलज्जं जिहासन्त्यपि बालकाः ।
विषूचीग्रस्तमिव तं जुगुप्सन्ते विवेकिनः ॥८५ ॥

madyapānād vītalajjaṁ jihāsanty api bālakāḥ ।
viṣūcīgrastam iva taṁ jugupsante vivekinaḥ ॥85 ॥

Even children prefer to get away from those who behave shamelessly due to drinking. The discriminate ones hate them as if diseased with cholera. [85]

मद्यकर्ता पूतिगन्धिः पटश्चास्य निकेतनम् ।
दुर्गन्धकलुषं तेन स्पृष्टं सर्वमपीदृशम् ॥८६ ॥

madyakartā pūtigandhiḥ paṭaś cāsya niketanam ।
durgandha-kaluṣaṁ tena spṛṣṭaṁ sarvam apīdṛśam ॥86 ॥

The maker of liquor smells badly and totally of it; his clothes also are felt so; so does his home; whatever he touches also becomes impure with the bad smell. [86]

मद्यासक्तं स्वस्य भार्या पिता माता सहोदरः ।
पुत्रोऽपि चेश्वरो द्वेष्टि तस्मान्मद्यं परित्यजेत् ॥८७ ॥

madyāsaktaṁ svasya bhāryā pitā mātā sahodaraḥ ।
putro 'pi ceśvaro dveṣṭi tasmān madyaṁ parityajet ॥87 ॥

His own wife, father, mother, brothers, children and even God, despise the alcoholic. Liquor, for this reason, is to be given up completely. [87]

इतीरितं साधुजनाभिनन्दितं
परोपकृत्यै लघुधर्मपञ्चकम् ।
इदं तदव्याहतमाचरन्ति ये
परं सुखं यान्ति परत्र चेह ते ॥८८ ॥

itīritaṁ sādhujanābhinanditaṁ
paropakṛtyai laghu-dharma-pañcakam,
idaṁ tad avyāhatam ācaranti ye
paraṁ sukhaṁ yānti paratra ceha te ॥88 ॥

Thus elucidated are the simple fivefold *dharmas*, always acclaimed by the noble-minded, for the benefit of all. Those who adhere to these undeterred, attain happiness both here and the hereafter. [88]

शुद्धिपञ्चकम्
(Fivefold Purities)

अथातः संप्रवक्ष्यामि संक्षेपाच्छुद्धिपञ्चकम् ।
शृणुध्वमवधानेन क्रमशः शुद्धितत्पराः ॥८९ ॥

athātaḥ saṁpravakṣyāmi saṁkṣepācchuddhipañcakam ।
śṛṇudhvam avadhānena kramaśaḥ śuddhitatparāḥ ॥89 ॥

Now I shall summarily tell you what the fivefold purities are, in their proper order. Listen to me carefully, O the ones much interested in purity. [89]

कायवाक्चेतसां शुद्धिरिन्द्रियाणां गृहस्य च ।
संक्षेपान्मर्त्यवर्गस्य पञ्चैताः शुद्धयः स्मृताः ॥९० ॥

kāyavākcetasāṁ śuddhir indriyāṇāṁ gṛhasya ca ।
saṁkṣepān martyavargasya pañcaitāḥ śuddhayaḥ śmṛtāḥ ॥90 ॥

The five purities, as far as the human race is concerned, are summarily understood as of the body, speech, mind, sense-organs and one's own residence. [90]

नित्यं शुद्धोदकस्नानं मलस्रोतो विशोधनम् ।
शुद्धिर्दन्तनखानां च शुद्धवस्त्रस्य धारणम् ॥९१ ॥

nityaṁ śuddhodaka-snānaṁ malasroto viśodhanam ।
śuddhir dantanakhānāṁ ca śuddhavastrasya dhāraṇam ॥91 ॥

शुद्धस्य वायोर्भोज्यस्य जलस्यापि निषेवणम् ।
करपादादि संशुद्धिर्देहशुद्धिरितीर्यते ॥९२ ॥

śuddhasya vāyor bhojyasya jalasyāpi niṣevaṇam ।
karapādādi saṁśuddhir dehaśuddhir itīryate ॥92 ॥

Bathing daily in clean water, giving clearance to dirt properly, keeping one's own teeth and nails clean, wearing clean clothes, ensuring that the air inhaled and the food and water consumed are clean, keeping one's own limbs such as hands and feet clean — these are said to constitute the bodily purity (*deha-śuddhi*). [91-92]

आवर्जकत्वं वर्णानां सुव्यक्तिः स्वरमाधुरी ।
पदानां स्फुटतौचित्यं लयोऽमी वचसो गुणाः ॥९३ ॥

āvarjakatvaṁ varṇānāṁ suvyaktiḥ svaramādhurī ।
padānāṁ sphuṭataucityaṁ layo 'mī vacaso guṇāḥ ॥93 ॥

Attractive pronunciation of syllables, their clarity, melodiousness of sound, explicitness of the words uttered, aptness of words and appealing harmony — these are the good qualities of speech. [93]

अनुद्वेजकता सत्यस्वाध्यायहितकीर्तनैः ।
सौष्ठवप्रियताभ्यां च नियतं वाग्विशुध्यति ॥९४ ॥

anudvejakatā satyasvādhyāyahitakīrtanaiḥ ।
sauṣṭhavapriyatābhyāṁ ca niyataṁ vāgviśudhyati ॥94 ॥

Not creating anxiety in others, being truthful, being conducive to self-learning, acclaiming whatever is favourable to all, nobility, being liked by all — these are the qualities that always make one's speech attain purity (*vāc śuddhi*). [94]

आर्जवं करुणा मैत्री मार्दवं च धृतिस्त्रपा ।
अद्वेषः प्रणिधानं च मनःशुद्धिं वितन्वते ॥९५ ॥

ārjavaṁ karuṇā maitrī mārdavaṁ ca dhr̥tis trapā ।
adveṣaḥ praṇidhānaṁ ca manaḥ śuddhiṁ vitanvate ॥95 ॥

Straightforwardness, kindness, being friendly, gentleness, firmness, bashfulness, angerlessness, meditativeness — these qualities result in one's mental purity (*manaḥ śuddhi*). [95]

अप्रियार्थेष्वप्रवृत्तिरपीडनमलालनम् ।
अयुक्तासंस्कृतश्चैतैः शुध्यतीन्द्रियपञ्चकम् ॥९६ ॥

apriyārtheṣv apravṛttir apīḍanam alālanam ।
ayuktāsaṁskṛtaś caitaiḥ śudhyatīndriyapañcakam ॥96 ॥

Not becoming involved in things that are not liked by you, neither torturing nor temptingly fondling the sense-organs, not glorifying anything not praiseworthy — keeping to these disciplines makes the five sense-organs purified (*indriya-śuddhi*). [96]

अन्तः सूर्यांशुसंपातः शुद्धवायुसमाश्रयः ।
अशुचिद्रव्यनिष्कासः सर्वतो नित्यमार्जनम् ॥९७ ॥

antaḥ sūryāṁśu-saṁpātaḥ śuddhavāyu-samāśrayaḥ ।
aśucidravyaniṣkāsaḥ sarvato nityamārjanam ॥97 ॥

पर्यन्ते मूत्रविष्टादेरनुत्सर्गः सुगन्धिभिः ।
सायं प्रातर्धूपनं च गृहशुद्धिकराणि षट् ॥९८ ॥

paryante mūtraviṣṭāder anutsargaḥ sugandhibhiḥ ।
sāyaṁ prātar dhūpanaṁ ca gṛhaśuddhikarāṇi ṣaṭ ॥98 ॥

The interior of the house having ample access to sun-light, having free flow of fresh air, discarding everything unclean, cleaning and sweeping the surroundings daily, not excreting in the surroundings, smoking incenses every morning and evening — these six habits help keep the house clean (*gṛha-śuddhi*). [97-98]

यः शुद्धिपञ्चकमिदं चरति प्रशस्त-
मारोग्यनित्यसुखहेतुकमात्मनीनम् ।
दीर्घायुरूर्जितवपुः सततप्रसन्न-
बुद्धिर्युवेव पुरुषो भवतीह लोके ॥९९ ॥

yaḥ śuddhipañcakam idaṁ carati praśasta-
mārogyanitya-sukhahetukamātmanīnam ।
dīrghāyur ūrjitavapuḥ satataprasanna-
buddhiryuveva puruṣo bhavatīha loke ॥99 ॥

The person who adheres to these celebrated fivefold purities that ensure good health and eternal happiness to oneself, lives a long life in this world with an energetic body and a constantly pleasant mind, as if a youth. [99]

चतुर्थः सर्गः (Canto Four)

सूतकम्
Childbirth

शिष्या ऊचुः —

भगवन् सर्वतत्त्वज्ञ सर्वप्राणिदयापर ।
भवतोदितमाकर्ण्य धर्मं सर्वमनोहरम् ॥१०० ॥

bhagavan sarvatattvajña sarvaprāṇi-dayāpara ।
bhavatoditam ākarṇya dharmaṁ sarvamanoharam ॥100 ॥

परं मुखरयत्यस्मान् जिज्ञासातः परस्य च ।
तस्मात् सूतिमुखान् धर्मान् व्यासेनोपदिशाधुना ॥१०१ ॥

paraṁ mukharayaty asmān jijñāsātaḥ parasya ca ।
tasmāt sūtimukhān dharmān vyāsenopadiśādhunā ॥101 ॥

The disciples said:

O Lord, the knower of the whole of the basic Truth, the one who is always kind-hearted to every living being, hearing from you the details of righteousness (*dharma*) in a telling manner, makes us desirous of knowing further, and it compels us to ask you about the details of the *dharma*s to be observed in childbirth and related matters. [100-101]

गुरुरुवाच —

शृणुध्वमवधानेन सदाचारपरायणाः ।
प्रसूतिविषयान् धर्मान् वक्ष्याम्यनतिविस्तरम् ॥१०२ ॥

śṛṇudhvam avadhānena sadācāraparāyaṇāḥ ।
prasūtiviṣayān dharmān vakṣyāmy anativistaram ॥102 ॥

O the ones fully devoted to virtuous behaviour patterns, now I shall tell you briefly what are the *dharmas* related to childbirth. Listen to me attentively. [102]

विशालं सूतिकावेश्म वायुसूर्यप्रकाशयोः ।
आदानप्रतिरोधार्थमनुकूलगवाक्षकम् ॥१०३ ॥

viśālaṁ sūtikāveśma vāyusūryaprakāśayoḥ ।
ādānapratirodhārtham anukūlagavākṣakam ॥103 ॥

The labour room should be a large one, having windows that allow in and keep out air and sunlight as are needed. [103]

तत्र प्रसूतिवैक्लव्यमापन्नायां तु जात्वपि ।
अस्वास्थ्यजनकं किञ्चिदप्यन्तर्न प्रवेशयेत् ॥१०४ ॥

tatra prasūtivaiklabyam āpannāyāṁ tu jātvapi ।
asvāsthyajanakaṁ kiñcid apy antar na praveśayet ॥104 ॥

Nothing that causes uneasiness in any way to the lady whose labour pain is already begun, should be let into that room. [104]

न केनापि प्रकारेण वैमनस्यकरं वचः ।
प्रकाशयेत् प्रसूतायाः पुरस्तान्नियतव्रता ॥१०५ ॥

na kenāpi prakāreṇa vaimanasyakaraṁ vacaḥ ।
prakāśayet prasūtāyāḥ purastān niyatavratā ॥105 ॥

गर्भसंग्रहणे दक्षा तद्विज्ञाने विचक्षणा ।
सदया समयाभिज्ञा शुचिः स्यात् साविकानिशम् ॥१०६ ॥

garbhasaṁgrahaṇe dakṣā tad vijñane vicakṣaṇā ।
sadayā samayābhijñā śuciḥ syāt sāvikāniśam ॥105 ॥

No word causing unhappiness to the lady in pain should be uttered therein. By her side should always be there a mid-wife, capable of self-restraint, expert in protecting the unborn child and knowledgeable in that field, kind-hearted, capable of acting as the situation demands, and of hygeinic habits. [105-106]

अनुरक्ताः बुद्धिमत्यः शौचाचारपरायणाः ।
परिचर्यासमर्थाश्च भवेयुः परिचारिकाः ॥१०७ ॥

anuraktāḥ buddhimatyaḥ śaucācāraparāyaṇāḥ ।
paricaryāsamarthāś ca bhaveyuḥ paricārikāḥ ॥107 ॥

The maid-servants around should be loving, intelligent, of clean and hygeinic habits, and skillful in doing services. [107]

भविता प्रसूताशौचशुद्धिरेकादशेऽहनि ।
आशौचान्ते शुद्धिकर्म पुण्यमन्यच्च कारयेत् ॥१०८ ॥

bhavitā prasūtāśaucaśuddhir ekādaśe 'hani ।
āśaucānte śuddhikarma puṇyam anyac ca kārayet ॥108 ॥

The purificatory rite related to childbirth is to be performed on the eleventh day. Once the period of impurity is over, other holy rites for attaining purities of other kinds also are to be performed. [108]

पक्षादुपरि कर्तव्यमर्वाङ्मासत्रयादपि ।
जातस्य नामकरणं तद्वन्निष्क्रमणं गृहात् ॥१०९ ॥

pakṣād upari kartavyam arvāṅ māsatrayād api ।
jātasya nāmakaraṇaṁ tadvan niṣkramaṇaṁ gṛhāt ॥109 ॥

Formal naming of the child (*nāmakaraṇa*) is to be done after a fortnight of the birth and not later than three months. Likewise, the rite of formally bringing the child outside the house (*niṣkramaṇa*) is also to be performed after three months. [109]

सुवचं सुश्रवं नामधेयमल्पाक्षरार्थवत् ।
अक्लिष्टं पुण्यनक्षत्रे विदधीत शुभेऽहनि ॥११० ॥

suvacaṁ suśravaṁ nāmadheyam alpākṣarārthavat ।
akliṣṭaṁ puṇyanakṣatre vidadhīta śubhe 'hani ॥110 ॥

The naming of the child is to be done on an auspicious day of holy constellation, and the name should be short, meaningful, easy to pronounce and sweet to hear. [110]

स्तनन्धयस्याल्पवह्नेरनुत्पन्नरदस्य च ।
षष्ठान्मासान्न कुर्वीत प्रागन्नप्राशनं शिशोः ॥१११ ॥

stanandhayasyālpavahner anutpannaradasya ca ।
ṣaṣṭhānmāsān na kurvīta prāg annaprāśanaṁ śiśoḥ ॥111 ॥

Do not do the rite of feeding the new-born child for the first time with heavy food (like cooked rice) — called *annaprāśana* — before it is six months old, in case breast feeding continues, proper digestive power is wanting, and the first teething has not happened. [111]

बालोपचरणम्
(Caring for the Child)

सौशील्याचारसंपन्ना नीरोगा करुणावती ।
प्रसादविनयोपेता योषिज्जातमुपाचरेत् ॥११२ ॥

sauśīlyācārasaṁpannā nīrogā karuṇāvatī ।
prasādavinayopetā yoṣij jātam upācaret ॥112 ॥

A woman of good character and ideal behaviour, healthy and kind-hearted, pleasant and humble, should care for the new-born child. [112]

विशुद्धमृदुवस्त्रेण स्वास्तीर्णे शयने शिशुम् ।
शाययेत् परितः शुद्धद्रव्यरम्ये गृहोदरे ॥११३ ॥

viśuddha-mṛduvastreṇa svāstīrṇe śayane śiśum ।
śāyayet paritaḥ śuddhadravyaramye gṛhodare ॥113 ॥

The child should be laid on a bed spread with soft and clean cloths, within a house decorated beautifully and cleanly. [113]

अनाशास्यं वचो द्रव्यममङ्गलनिवेदनम् ।
अवमाननमाटोपं न बालस्य प्रकाशयेत् ॥११४ ॥

anāśāsyaṁ vaco dravyam amaṅgala-nivedanam ।
avamānanam āṭopaṁ na bālasya prakāśayet ॥114 ॥

Undesirable words should not be uttered in the presence of the child. So too, offering inauspicious things is to be avoided. To be insolent towards someone and showing self-conceit also should not find expression in the presence of the child. [114]

आपञ्चमाब्दं धात्र्यैव लालनाचोदनादिभिः।
उपाख्यानेन महतां प्रतिच्छन्दावलोकतः ॥११५॥

āpañcamābdaṁ dhātryaiva lālanā-codanādibhiḥ ।
upākhyānena mahatāṁ praticchandāvalokataḥ ॥115॥

व्यक्ताक्षरेण वचसा शुद्धवासो विभूषणैः।
भोज्येन शुचिना बालो वर्धनीयः प्रयत्नतः ॥११६॥

vyaktākṣareṇa vacasā śuddhavāso vibhūṣaṇaiḥ ।
bhojyena śucinā bālo vardhanīyaḥ prayatnataḥ ॥116॥

The child is to be diligently nurtured by the nurse herself for five years, by fondling, invigorating, narrating the stories of great people, showing attractive images and pictures, talking with clearly pronounced words, adorning with clean clothes and ornaments, and feeding on pure and healthy food. [115-116]

विद्यारंभम्
(Initiation into Formal Education)

एवं प्रवर्धमानस्य विद्यारंभं शुभोत्तरम्।
पूर्वं तु पञ्चमादब्दात् कारयेदात्मवेदिभिः ॥११७॥

evaṁ pravardhamānasya vidyāraṁbhaṁ śubhottaram ।
pūrvaṁ tu pañcamād abdāt kāryed ātmavedibhiḥ ॥117॥

The child growing up thus, before attaining five years, should be initiated into formal education in an auspicious and noble way, by knowers of the Self. [117]

विदुषा भक्तियुक्तेन करुणामृदुचेतसा।
वृत्ताचारवता कार्यमक्षरारंभणं शिशोः ॥११८॥

viduṣā bhaktiyuktena karuṇā-mṛducetasā ।
vṛttācāravatā kāryam akṣarārambhaṇaṁ śiśoḥ ॥118 ॥

The initiation of the child to the first letters should be officiated by someone who is well learned, who is fully devout, who is kindly and tender-hearted, and who is of good manners. [118]

कृतस्नानं शुचिं बालं विधाय प्राङ्मुखं गुरोः ।
ध्यात्वा जिह्वाञ्चले तस्य सुवर्णेन लिखेन्मनुं ॥११९ ॥

kṛtasnānaṁ śuciṁ bālaṁ vidhāya prāṅmukhaṁ guroḥ ।
dhyātvā jihvāñcale tasya suvarṇena likhen manuṁ ॥119 ॥

Having bathed well and made bodily clean, the child should be seated facing the *guru*, who should meditatively write the sacred charm (*mantra*) at the tip of his tongue, with gold. [119]

वर्णानुच्चारयित्वाथ प्रणतं बालकं गुरुः ।
आशीर्वदेत् प्रसन्नात्मा तस्य श्रेयोऽभिवृधये ॥१२० ॥

varṇān uccārayitvātha praṇataṁ bālakaṁ guruḥ ।
āśīrvadet prasannātmā tasya śreyo 'bhivṛdhaye ॥120 ॥

The child should then be made to pronounce the words of the *mantra*. Then the *guru* should bless the child who prostrates before him, wishing for a good future, spiritually and worldly. [120]

पञ्चमः सर्गः (Canto Five)

आश्रमधर्मम्
(Duties Related to Each Stage of Life)

शिष्या ऊचुः —

ज्ञातृज्ञानज्ञेयतत्त्वनीतिव्याख्यविचक्षण ।
अख्यातं भवता यद्यद् वाक्यं वाक्यविशारद ॥१२१ ॥

jñatṛ-jñāna-jñeya-tattva nītivyākhya-vicakṣaṇa ।
akhyātaṁ bhavatā yadyad vākyaṁ vākyaviśārada ॥121 ॥

अस्माभिरवधानेन श्रुतं तल्लोकसम्मतम् ।
अथाश्रमस्वरूपं च साधुजिज्ञास्यतेऽधुना ॥१२२ ॥

asmābhir avdhānena śrutaṁ tal lokasammatam ।
athāśramasvarūpaṁ ca sādhu jijñāsyate 'dhunā ॥122 ॥

The disciples said:

O the one clear-sighted in elucidating the basics of the knower, the knowledge and the known, as well as of pure justice, O the one proficient in the apt usage of words, the words we have been listening to with full attention are agreeable to the entire world. And now we wish to know properly the nature of *āśramas* (varying stages of human life). [122]

गुरुरुवाच —

अथाहं संप्रवक्ष्यामि ज्ञातव्यानाश्रमांस्तथा ।
तेषां सामान्यधर्मांश्च क्रमशः शृणुतास्तिकाः ॥१२३ ॥

athāhaṁ saṁpravakṣyāmi jñātavyān āśramāṁs tathā ।
teṣāṁ sāmānyadharmāṅś ca kramaśaḥ śṛṇutāstikāḥ ॥123 ॥

The Guru said:

O the faithful ones, now I shall tell you about the *āśrama*s (varying stages in human life) in their order in general, and also about the duties of humans in those stages. Listen to me. [123]

पूर्वाचार्याः ब्रह्मचर्यं गार्हस्थ्यं च ततः परम् ।
वानप्रस्थं च संन्यासं आश्रामांश्चतुरो जगुः ॥१२४ ॥

pūrvācāryāḥ brahmacaryaṁ gārhasthyaṁ ca tataḥ param ।
vānaprasthaṁ ca saṁnyāsaṁ āśrāmāṁś caturo jaguḥ ॥124 ॥

The ancient masters glorify the *āśrama*s as four: *brahmacarya* (the life of a spiritual student), *gārhasthya* (the life of a householder), *vānaprastha* (the life of a hemit living in forests) and *saṁnyāsa* (the life of a renunciate). [124]

तथाप्यवहितप्रज्ञाः कालेऽस्मिन्नाश्रमास्त्रयः ।
पर्याप्ता एवमेवासंस्त्रयः कालेऽपि वैदिके ॥१२५ ॥

tathāpy avahitaprajñāḥ kāle 'sminn āśramās trayaḥ ।
paryāptā evam evāsaṁs trayaḥ kāle 'pi vaidike ॥125 ॥

Yet, O the ones of attentive mind, three *āśrama*s are enough in modern times. Even in the ancient Vedic times did these three alone practically exist. [125]

ते ब्रह्मचर्यगार्हस्थ्य संन्यासा इति मे मतिः ।
तेषां सामान्यरूपाणि संक्षिप्यादौ निरूप्यते ॥१२६ ॥

te brahmacarya-gārhasthya saṁnyāsā iti me matiḥ ।
teṣāṁ sāmānyarūpāṇi saṁkṣipyādau nirūpyate ॥126 ॥

These three, in my opinion, are *brahmacarya* (studenthood), *gārhasthya* (householder-hood), and *saṁnyāsa* (to be a full renunciate). We shall now summarily think of the general nature of these three. [126]

विद्यारंभात् परं पुंसश्चतुर्विंशवयोऽवधि ।
ब्रह्मचर्यं बालिकायाः स्यात् षोडशवयोऽवधि ॥१२७ ॥

vidyārambhāt paraṁ puṁsaś caturviṁśavayo 'vadhi ।
brahmacaryaṁ bālikāyāḥ syāt ṣoḍaśavayo 'vadhi ॥126 ॥

After the initiation into formal education, a boy should observe *brahmacarya* till he is twenty-four. In the case of a girl it is to be observed till sixteen. [127]

विहितब्रह्मचर्यान्ते गृहित्वं यदि वाञ्छति ।
उत्सृजेत् ब्रह्मचर्यं तदन्यथा न परित्यजेत् ॥१२८ ॥

vihitabrahmacaryānte gṛhitvaṁ yadi vāñchati ।
utsṛjet brahmacaryaṁ tad anyathā na parityajet ॥128 ॥

If one, at the end of the customary *brahmacarya*, wants to become a householder, then he should give up *brahmacarya*; otherwise he should not do so. [128]

पुरुषो यदि षट्त्रिंशद् वयोन्तं ब्रह्मचर्यवान् ।
तथैव वनिता त्रिंशद् वयोऽन्तं ब्रह्मचारिणी ॥१२९ ॥

puruṣo yadi ṣaṭtriṁśad vayontaṁ brahmacaryavān ।
tathaiva vanitā triṁśad vayo 'ntaṁ brahmacāriṇī ॥129 ॥

(In the latter case), a man should remain *brahmacārin* till thirty-six, and a woman till thirty. [129]

अविच्छिन्नब्रह्मचर्यप्रशस्तमतिशालिनौ ।
नेतृत्वमर्हतस्तौ तु जनतापर्यवेक्षणे ॥१३० ॥

avicchinna-brahmacarya-praśasta-matiśālinau ।
netṛttvam arhatastau tu janatāparyavekṣaṇe ॥130 ॥

Both, having praiseworthy knowledge supported by unbroken *brahmacarya*, become leaders who look after the well-being of the society. [130]

स्वधर्मं संविधायैव गार्हस्थ्याद् विनिवर्तयेत् ।
संपूर्णषष्टिवर्षश्चेत् संन्यसेत् स्वेच्छया ततः ॥१३१ ॥

svadharmaṁ saṁvidhāyaiva gārhasthyād vinivartayet ।
saṁpūrṇaṣaṣṭivarṣaś cet saṁnyaset svecchayā tataḥ ॥131 ॥

After having fulfilled all one's duties related to a householder, one should withdraw oneself from being a *gṛhastha*, and after sixty, one is to take to *saṁnyāsa* on one's own. [131]

अनुष्ठाय ब्रह्मचर्यं गार्हस्थ्यं च यथाविधि ।
सदारो यस्त्यजेद्देहं प्राज्ञोऽयमृषिरिष्यते ॥१३२ ॥

anuṣṭhāya brahmacaryaṁ gārhasthyaṁ ca yathāvidhi ।
sadāro yastyajed dehaṁ prājño'yam ṛṣir iṣyate ॥132 ॥

After having undergone the discipline of *brahmacarya*, and after having lived the life of a householder along with the wife according to customary rules, the man of wisdom who gives up the body is called a *ṛṣi* or seer. [132]

निष्कामकर्मनिरते जगतः सेवने हि या ।
या च मोक्षे विहायैते न यतीनां स्पृहोचिता ॥१३३ ॥

niṣkāmakarmanirate jagataḥ sevane hi yā ।
yā ca mokṣe vihāyaite na yatīnāṁ spṛhocitā ॥133 ॥

No motive other than doing service to the world by being engaged in activities not motivated by personal gains as well as attaining final liberation (*mokṣa*), is desirable for *yati*s (persons of full self-restraint). [133]

कर्मबन्धविनिर्मुक्त्यै नास्त्युपायो महत्तरः ।
तदेकान्तसुखापेक्षी कर्म निष्काममाचरेत् ॥१३४ ॥

karmabandhavinirmuktyai nāsty upāyo mahattaraḥ ।
tad ekāntasukhāpekṣī karma niṣkāmam ācaret ॥134 ॥

No better way is forthcoming for attaining liberation from all bondages caused by actions (*karma-bandha*s). Those who aim at the one-pointed ultimate happiness, therefore, should resort to desireless actions (*niṣkāma-karma*s). [134]

बहुधाऽपि विभक्तं तत् साधुमानवजीवितम् ।
तत्तदाश्रमसंबद्धा विधयो विविधा अपि ॥१३५ ॥

bahudhā 'pi vibhaktaṁ tat sādhumānavajīvitam ।
tat tad āśramasaṁbaddhā vidhayo vividhā api ॥135 ॥

Virtuous human life naturally can be of various kinds. Accordingly, injunctions related to *āśrama*s also do vary. [135]

दिवाकृतं तमिस्रायां मासेष्वष्टसु यत्कृतम् ।
वृष्टावपि सुखायैवं कृतं बाल्ये तु यौवने ॥१३६ ॥

divākṛtaṁ tamisrāyāṁ māseṣvaṣṭasu yat kṛtam ।
vṛṣṭāvapi sukhāyaivaṁ kṛtaṁ bālye tu yauvane ॥136 ॥

What one does at daytime ensures happiness at night; what one does during the eight brighter months ensures happiness during the four rainy months. Likewise, what one does in childhood ensures happiness at youth. [136]

तारुण्ये विहितं यत्तद् वार्धक्ये च सुखाप्तये ।
आमृतेरखिला वृत्तिः स्यादुत्तरसुखाय च ॥१३७ ॥

tāruṇye vihitaṁ yat tad vārdhakye ca sukhāptaye ।
āmṛter akhilā vṛttiḥ syād uttarasukhāya ca ॥137 ॥

What one does when a youth brings in happiness at old-age. The activities one is engaged in till the end of life ensures the happiness thereafter. [137]

यथावदाश्रमविधीन् समनुष्ठितवान् पुमान् ।
सोऽयमेवेति विज्ञेयो लोकतत्त्वार्थवेदिभिः ॥१३८ ॥

yathāvad āśramavidhīn samanuṣṭhitavān pumān ।
so 'yam eveti vijñeyo lokatattvārthavedibhiḥ ॥138 ॥

One who lives fully adhering to the injunctions concerning *āśrama*s alone is well-known as 'human' (*pumān*) amongst those who know the basic Reality about the world. [138]

षष्ठः सर्गः (Canto Six)

ब्रह्मचर्यम्
(Studenthood)

शिष्या ऊचुः —

आश्रमाणां तु सामान्यस्वरूपं गुरुणा क्रमात् ।
उपदिष्टं निशम्यैव संतुष्यामो यतीश्वर ॥१३९ ॥

āśramāṇāṁ tu sāmānyasvarūpaṁ guruṇā kramāt ।
upadiṣṭaṁ niśamyaiva saṁtuṣyāmo yatīśvara ॥139 ॥

The disciples said:

O the lord among *yatis*, we are all extremely happy on hearing the overall nature of the *āśramas* taught in their order by you, the *guru*. [139]

तथाऽपि तेषां प्रत्येकं विशेषानपि तत्त्वतः ।
शुश्रूषा नः प्रसादेन तत्प्रकाश्यानुशाधि नः ॥१४० ॥

tathā 'pi teṣāṁ pratyekaṁ viśeṣān api tattvataḥ ।
śuśrūṣā naḥ prasādena tat prakāśyānuśādhi naḥ ॥140 ॥

Still we are inquisitive to know from you the details of each of the *āśramas*. With a pleasant mind, please instruct us making it clear. [140]

गुरुरुवाच —

श्रुणुत प्रीतिसंपन्ना ब्रह्मचर्यव्रतं शिवम् ।
आश्रमाणां प्रधानत्वात् प्रथमं तन्निगद्यते ॥१४१ ॥

śṛuṇuta prītisaṁpannā brahmacaryavrataṁ śivam ।
āśramāṇāṁ pradhānatvāt prathamaṁ tan nigadyate ॥141 ॥

The Guru said:

O the ones rich in contentment, hear from me now about the auspicious discipline of *brahmacarya*. It is thought of as "the first" of the *āśrama*s because of its importance. [141]

गर्भे विरूढमात्रस्य ब्रह्मचर्यं भवेच्छिशोः ।
तदर्थं ब्रह्मचर्येण वर्तेत जननी तदा ॥१४२॥

garbhe virūḍhamātrasya brahmacaryaṁ bhavecchiśoḥ ।
tad arthaṁ brahmacaryeṇa varteta jananī tadā ॥142॥

A child has to remain in *brahmacarya* from the very moment he or she gets formulated as an embryo in the womb. The mother, for this reason, should observe *brahmacarya* throughout the carrying period. [142]

शिशोर्गुरुकुलप्राप्तिपर्यन्तं परिचारिका ।
पितरावपि तस्यैतां स्मरेयुर्ब्रह्मचारिताम् ॥१४३॥

śiśor gurukulapraptiparyantaṁ paricārikā ।
pitarāvapi tasyaitāṁ smareyur brahmacāritām ॥143॥

A child, till the time he or she is taken to the *gurukula* (for formal education), should be reminded of the importance of his or her being a *brahmacārin* by both the parents and the maid-servant. [143]

आपञ्चमाब्दं प्रेम्णैव शिशुं देवमिवाचरेत् ।
तावत्तद् बुद्धिसंस्कारं कुर्वीत जननी स्वयम् ॥१४४॥

āpañcamābdaṁ premṇaiva śiśuṁ devam ivācaret ।
tāvat tad buddhisaṁskāraṁ kurvīta jananī svayam ॥144॥

Till five years old, the child should be lovingly treated like a god. The job of nurturing the child intellectually till then is to be done by the mother herself. [144]

पितरौ पुत्रसंभूतिं आकांक्षन्तौ निजात्मजम् ।
अक्षरारंभणादूर्ध्वं वासयेतां गुरोः कुले ॥१४५॥

pitarau putrasaṁbhūtiṁ ākāṅkṣantau nijātmajam ।
akṣarāraṁbhaṇād ūdhvaṁ vāsayetāṁ guroḥ kule ॥145 ॥

The parents who are desirous of the well-being of the child should let their son live in a *gurukula* after initiation into formal education (*vidyārambham*). [145]

आकांक्षन् जीवितोत्कर्षम् वर्णी गुरुकुले वसेत् ।
निर्णीतकालपर्यन्तम् गुर्वाज्ञां परिपालयन् ॥१४६ ॥

ākāṅkṣan jīvitotkarṣaṁ varṇī gurukule vaset ।
nirṇītakālaparyantam gurvājñāṁ paripālayan ॥146 ॥

Desirous of attaining eminence in life, a student should live in the *gurukula* complying with the orders of the *guru*. [146]

वर्णिनः पितरौ निःस्वौ यदि देशसभा स्वयम् ।
ब्रह्मचर्याव्रतं सम्यगवश्यं तस्य निर्वहेत् ॥१४७ ॥

varṇinaḥ pitarau niḥsvau yadi deśasabhā svayam ।
brahmacaryāvrataṁ samyag avaśyaṁ tasya nirvahet ॥147 ॥

If both the parents of the student are too poor, the studenthood should be taken care of by the local public body on its own. [147]

वसन् गुरुकुले वर्णी गन्तुकामो निजालयम् ।
साचार्यो नियते काले गच्छेत् गुरुपरायणः ॥१४८ ॥

vasan gurukule varṇī gantukāmo nijālayam ।
sācāryo niyate kāle gacchet guruparāyaṇaḥ ॥148 ॥

If a *brahmacārin*, living fully devoted to the *guru* in a *gurukula*, wishes to visit his house, he should do so only along with the *guru* at a previously fixed time. [148]

शिक्षयेच्छिष्यमाचार्यः शौचमादौ विशेषतः ।
तथा गुरुकुलाचारान् सर्वानपि शुभोत्तरान् ॥१४९ ॥

śikṣayec chiṣyam ācāryaḥ śaucam ādau viśeṣataḥ ।
tathā gurukulācārān sarvān api śubhottarān ॥149 ॥

The first thing the teacher should teach his student specifically is how to observe purities. The other good manners and behaviour patterns of the *gurukula* should also likewise be taught. [149]

आचारमाचरेन्नित्यं उपासीत यथाविधि ।
द्वे सन्ध्ये वीततन्द्रीकं ब्रह्मचारी यतेन्द्रियः ॥१५० ॥

ācāram ācaren nityaṁ upāsīta yathāvidhi ।
dve sandhye vītatandrīkaṁ brahmacārī yatendriyaḥ ॥150 ॥

The customary disciplines of adoration should be practised by the *brahmacārin* of self-restraint with no hesitation, both in the morning and evening, as is enjoined in the scriptures. [150]

उपक्रान्त्युपसंहृत्योः पाठस्याचार्यमादरात् ।
शिष्योऽभिवादयेदेव विनीतो विधिपूर्वकम् ॥१५१ ॥

upakrāntyupasaṁhṛtyoḥ pāṭhasyācāryam ādarāt ।
śiṣyo 'bhivādayed eva vinīto vidhipūrvakam ॥151 ॥

The disciple should respectfully salute the master in the customary way with all humility, before and after each lesson. [151]

गुरोस्सकाशान्नियतं इहामुत्र शुभावहाः ।
अध्येतव्याः समा विद्याः तत्त्वज्ञानाय धीमता ॥१५२ ॥

guros sakāśān niyataṁ ihāmutraśubhāvahāḥ ।
adhyetavyāḥ samā vidyāḥ tattvajñānāya dhīmatā ॥152 ॥

An intelligent disciple, in order to know the ultimate Reality, should invariably learn everything that is conducive to happiness here as well as hereafter, from the *guru*. [152]

श्रद्धावान् ब्रह्मचारी तु प्रस्तुतं धर्मपञ्चकम् ।
अनुस्मरेच्चानुतिष्ठेत् तथा तच्छुद्धिपञ्चकम् ॥१५३ ॥

śraddhāvān brahmacārī tu prastutaṁ dharmapañcakam ।
anusmarec cānutiṣṭhet tathā tacchuddhipañcakam ॥153 ॥

The faithful *brahmacārin*, on his part, should always be mindful of and practise the previously mentioned fivefold *dharmas* (righteousnesses) as well as the fivefold purities (*śuddhis*). [153]

बलादावर्जकार्थेषु चलच्चेतो निरोधयेत् ।
विना तन्निग्रहं काष्ठां पुरुषो नाधिगच्छति ॥१५४ ॥

balād āvarjakārtheṣu calac ceto nirodhayet ।
vinā tan nigrahaṁ kāṣṭhāṁ puruṣo nādhigacchati ॥154 ॥

Mind is to be restrained from captivating objects of pleasure. No man attains his final goal without self-restraint. [154]

इन्द्रियाणामेकतमं यद्यन्यत्र प्रवर्तते ।
प्रज्ञाऽपि तेन निर्गत्य व्रतभंगाय कल्पते ॥१५५ ॥

indriyāṇām ekatamaṁ yady anyatra pravartate ।
prajñā 'pi tena nirgatya vratabhaṅgāya kalpate ॥155 ॥

In case any one of the sense-organs goes astray, then the mind also goes after it. This results in one's breaking of the careful observance of *brahmacarya*. [155]

तदिन्द्रियाणि समये बुद्धिमानुपरोधयेत् ।
इन्द्रियोपरमः सत्यं तपोवर्त्मनि संश्रयः ॥१५६ ॥

tad indriyāṇi samaye buddhimān uparodhayet ।
indriyoparamaḥ satyaṁ tapo vartmani saṁśrayaḥ ॥156 ॥

An intelligent one, therefore, should restrain the senses at proper time. Restraining the sense-organs is what is to be resorted to by those who follow the path of austere seekers. [156]

निष्कासयेद् गुरुकुलाद् दुर्विनीतमनाश्रवम् ।
ब्रह्मचारिणमन्येषां दुःसंसर्गनिवृत्तये ॥१५७ ॥

niṣkāsayed gurukulād durvinītam anāśravam ।
brahmacāriṇam anyeṣāṁ duḥsaṁsarganivṛttaye ॥157 ॥

A *brahmacārin* who does not listen to the *guru* and is not at all humble, for the sake of avoiding ill-effects on other students, should be expelled from the *gurukula*. [157]

अविशेषेण पितरावाचार्यश्च कृपाबलात् ।
पोषेऽधिकारिणस्तस्य स्थूल सूक्ष्मशरीरयोः ॥१५८ ॥

aviśeṣeṇa pitarāv ācāryaś ca kṛpābalāt ।
poṣe 'dhikāriṇas tasya sthūla sūkṣmaśarirayoḥ ॥158 ॥

The parents as well as the *guru* are equally responsible for nourishing compassionately both the gross body and the subtle body of the *brahmacārin*. [158]

वदेत् सत्यं चरेत् धर्मं स्वाध्यायं नित्यमाचरेत् ।
कुशलात् सत्यधर्माभ्यां न प्रमाद्येद् विभूतये ॥१५९ ॥

vadet satyaṁ caret dharmaṁ svādhyāyaṁ nityam ācaret ।
kuśalāt satyadharmābhyāṁ na pramādyed vibhūtaye ॥159 ॥

He should tell truth (*satya*), and should behave in accordance with *dharma*; self-learning should be constantly practised. For the sake of ensuring well-being, he should make no error of omission in respect of what ensures well-being (*kuśala*) as well as *satya* and *dharma*. [159]

दैवपैतृककर्माणि न प्रमादेन लंघयेत् ।
सदाऽऽचार्यपित्रातिथीन् अनुवर्तेत देववत् ॥१६० ॥

daivapaitṛka-karmāṇi na pramādena laṅghayet ।
sadā ''cāryapitrātithīn anuvarteta devavat ॥160 ॥

The rituals related to gods and ancestors should not be transgressed by mistake. One's own master, parents and guests are to be treated and honoured as god-like. [160]

सतामाचारोपदेशौ गृणीयात् पुण्यकर्मवत् ।
ब्रह्मचर्यं तपो नूनं विद्याभ्यासाय कल्पते ॥१६१ ॥

satām ācāropadeśau gr̥ṇīyāt puṇyakarmavat ।
brahmacaryaṁ tapo nūnaṁ vidyābhyāsāya kalpate ॥161 ॥

The instructions and manners of those who are virtuous and respectable should inspire him like meritorious deeds (*puṇya-karmas*). *Brahmacarya* and *tapas* (austere self-discipline), for certain, always go with education. [161]

मितनिद्रा मिताहारो मितवस्त्रपरिग्रहः ।
मितभाषणमेकैकं भूषणं ब्रह्मचारिणः ॥१६२ ॥

mitanidrā mitāhāro mitavastraparigrahaḥ ।
mitabhāṣaṇam ekaikaṁ bhūṣaṇaṁ brahmacāriṇaḥ ॥162 ॥

Sleeping moderately, eating moderately, dressing oneself moderately, moderate talk — these separately become adornments to a *brahmacārin*. [162]

द्यूतं पैशुन्यमनृतं अपवादवचस्तथा ।
कामक्रोधावथालस्यं असूयां च परित्यजेत् ॥१६३ ॥

dyūtaṁ paiśunyam anr̥taṁ apavādavacas tathā ।
kāmakrodhāvathālasyaṁ asūyāṁ ca parityajet ॥163 ॥

Gambling, slandering, being untruthful, spreading scandals, lust, anger, laziness, jealousy — all these are to be totally given up by a *brahmacārin*. [163]

उषस्येव समुत्थाय स्नात्वा देवमनुस्मरन् ।
प्रातःसन्ध्यामुपास्यान्ते स्वाध्यायनिरतो भवेत् ॥१६४ ॥

uṣasy eva samutthāya snātvā devam anusmaran ।
prātaḥ sandhyām upāsyānte svādhyāyanirato bhavet ॥164 ॥

The *brahmacārin* should get up in the early morning, and after taking bath, should make the morning prayers contemplating on God. He should then become engaged in self-learning. [164]

एवं वर्णी सायमपि विदधीत विधिक्रमम् ।
निरीक्षेत श्रद्दधानः पाठकाले गुरोर्मुखम् ॥१६५ ॥

evaṁ varṇī sāyam api vidadhīta vidhikramam ।
nirīkṣeta śraddadhānaḥ pāṭhakāle guror mukham ॥165 ॥

Likewise should the *brahmacārin* do what he is supposed to do at dusk also according to accepted precepts. The student should be looking at the face of the *guru* while he gives lessons. [165]

तपस्या फलिता भूयाद् अवश्यं ब्रह्मचारिणः ।
वरिवस्या प्रसन्ना चेत् पितृमातृगुरुत्रयी ॥१६६ ॥

tapasyā phalitā bhūyād avaśyaṁ brahmacāriṇaḥ ।
varivasyā prasannā cet pitṛmātṛgurutrayī ॥166 ॥

A *brahmacārin*'s austere self-discipline (*tapasyā*) and adoration (*varivasyā*) could be treated as having become fruitful if his father, mother and *guru* are pleased with these. [166]

नियतब्रह्मचर्यान्ते न गार्हस्थ्यं यदीहते ।
आजीवमोचनं वर्णी सुखं गुरुकुले वसेत् ॥१६७ ॥

niyatabrahmacaryānte na gārhasthyaṁ yadīhate ।
ājīvamocanaṁ varṇī sukhaṁ gurukule vaset ॥167 ॥

If he does not wish to have a householder's life at the end of the prescribed period of *brahmacarya*, then he should live happily in the *gurukula* itself till the end of his life. [167]

अनवाप्य गुरोर्मातुः पितुश्चानुमतिं पुमान् ।
यद्युद्वहेद् यथाकामं धर्मात् स प्रच्युतो भवेत् ॥१६८ ॥

anavāpya guror mātuḥ pituścānumatiṁ pumān ।
yady udvahed yathākāmaṁ dharmāt sa pracyuto bhavet ॥168 ॥

The man who gets married as he wishes, without getting the approval of the *guru*, mother and father, is to be treated as having fallen from *dharma*.

शिष्या ऊचुः —

आख्यातो भवता धर्मो विशेषाद् ब्रह्मचारिणः ।
आदितो यः श्रुतोऽस्माभिः सर्वलोकोपकारकः ॥१६९॥

ākhyāto bhavatā dharmo viśeṣād brahmacāriṇaḥ ।
ādito yaḥ śruto 'smābhiḥ sarvalokopakārakaḥ ॥169॥

The disciples said:

We have been listening to the specific *dharma* of *brahmacārin*s narrated by you, from its very beginning. This, of course, is beneficial to the entire world. [169]

सप्तमः सर्गः (Canto Seven)

गार्हस्थ्यम्
(Being a Householder)

अथातः करुणामूर्त्ते गृहिणोऽपि विशेषतः ।
धर्मान् सविस्तरं ब्रूहि नित्यकल्याणहेतुकान् ॥१७० ॥

athātaḥ karuṇāmūrte gṛhiṇo 'pi viśeṣataḥ ।
dharmān savistaraṁ brūhi nityakalyāṇahetukān ॥170 ॥

O the embodiment of compassion, now therefore, tell us about the specific *dharma*s of householders in detail. These *dharma*s, we know, are causal to the eternal well-being of humanity. [170]

गुरुरुवाच —

शृणुतातःपरं वच्मि गृहस्थस्य विधिक्रमम् ।
त्रिवर्गनिलयं साक्षात् मुक्तिद्वारमपावृतम् ॥१७१ ॥

śṛṇutātaḥ paraṁ vacmi gṛhasthasya vidhikramam ।
trivarga-nilayaṁ sākṣāt muktidvāram apāvṛtam ॥171 ॥

The Guru said:

Now I shall tell you about the precepts related to the duties of householders. These duties really constitute the repository of the threefold human values — *trivarga*, i.e., *dharma* (righteousness), *artha* (wealth) and *kāma* (desire for enjoyments) — and form the doorway opening towards the real final liberation (*mukti*) or *parama-puruṣārtha* (the ultimate goal of life). Listen to me. [171]

वेदानधीत्य निखिलान् तत्तदाचार्यकल्पितान् ।
पित्रोर्गुरोश्चानुमत्या स्नातः साधु गृही भवेत् ॥१७२ ॥

vedān adhītya nikhilān tat tad ācāryakalpitān ।
pitror guroś cānumatyā snātaḥ sādhu gṛhī bhavet ॥172 ॥

Having learnt all the Vedas (sciences) as directed by the master, he should purify himself by formal bathing, and then, with the permission of the parents and *guru*, should become a good householder. [172]

उत्तमाभिजनां धर्म्यां सुशीलां लक्षणान्विताम् ।
प्रसन्नां वरयेत् कन्यां गुरुमातृपितृप्रियाम् ॥१७३ ॥

uttamābhijanāṁ dharmyāṁ suśīlāṁ lakṣaṇānvitām ।
prasannāṁ varayet kanyāṁ gurumātṛpitṛpriyām ॥173 ॥

Born of a noble family, the bride should be willing to abide by the *dharmas*, should be of ideal habits, should be having all the best marks of womanly nature, should be pleasant, and should be liked by the *guru*, mother and father. [173]

तया दयितया धर्मं आचरेन्नियतेन्द्रियः ।
धर्माय जीवनं नूनं प्रजायै च गृहव्रतम् ॥१७४ ॥

tayā dayitayā dharmaṁ ācaren niyatendriyaḥ ।
dharmāya jīvanaṁ nūnaṁ prajāyai ca gṛhavratam ॥174 ॥

Along with that wife, one should practise *dharma* with restrained sense-organs. Human life should be for upholding *dharma*. And observing a householder's duty should be for the sake of progeny. [174]

दानाय धनसंपत्तिर्गार्हस्थ्ये विहिता हिता ।
अतिथ्यगतिभैक्षार्थं पचेन्नैवात्मकारणात् ॥१७५ ॥

dānāya dhanasaṁpattir gārhasthye vihitā hitā ।
atithyagatibhaikṣārthaṁ pacen naivātmakāraṇāt ॥175 ॥

Accumulation of wealth by a householder should rather be meant for distributing as gifts. Cooking is to be done at home meant mainly for feeding guests and destitutes, and never for oneself alone. [175]

प्रणयः सर्वभूतेषु करुणामसृणा मतिः ।
समत्वं सर्वभावेषु भवेयुर्गृहिणो गुणाः ॥१७६ ॥

praṇayaḥ sarvabhūteṣu karuṇāmasṛṇā matiḥ ।
samatvaṁ sarvabhāveṣu bhaveyur gṛhiṇo guṇāḥ ॥176 ॥

Love for all living beings, a mind filled with compassion, equality towards everything — these would be the ideal qualities of a householder. [176]

यती वर्णी चातिथिश्च पक्वान्नःस्वामिनो मताः ।
यतिहस्ते जलं दत्वा भक्ष्यं दद्यात्ततो जलम् ॥१७७ ॥

yatī varṇī cātithiś ca pakvānnaḥsvāmino matāḥ ।
yatihaste jalaṁ datvā bhakṣyaṁ dadyāt tato jalam ॥177 ॥

It is held that *saṁnyāsins*, *brahmacārins* and guests are the real owners of the food cooked by a householder. A *saṁnyāsin* should be welcomed to eat by pouring water at his hands. Water is again to be offered after his eating. [177]

उद्वाहार्थं गुरुकुलान्निर्धार्येतां वधूवरौ ।
तत्कर्म तत्र कार्यं वा जानता देवतालये ॥१७८ ॥

udvāhārthaṁ gurukulān nirdhāryetāṁ vadhūvarau ।
tat karma tatra kāryaṁ vā jānatā devatālaye ॥178 ॥

It is better to find out the bride and the bridegroom for marriage, from the same *gurukula*. The ceremony is to be performed either at the *gurukula* or at a temple, and is to be officiated by a knowledgeable person. [178]

वरस्य पितरौ वध्वाः पितरौ सहपाठिनौ ।
वधूवरज्ञातियुग्मं आचार्यश्च पुरोहितः ॥१७९ ॥

varasya pitarau vadhvāḥ pitarau sahapāṭhinau ।
vadhūvarajñātiyugmaṁ ācāryaśca purohitaḥ ॥179 ॥

दशसन्निदधीरंस्ते पाणिपीडणकर्मणि ।
नातो न्यूनास्तु युज्येरन् लोकसंग्रहकारणात् ॥१८० ॥

daśasannidadhīraṁste pāṇipīḍaṇakarmaṇi ।
nāto nyūnāstu yujyeran lokasaṁgraha-kāraṇāt ॥180 ॥

The two parents of the bridegroom, the two parents of the bride, two classmates, two close relatives of the bride and the groom, the *guru* and the priest — these ten should be present at the marriage ceremony, and the number of participants should never be lesser. It is in view of the well-being of human society that such a system is introduced. [179-180]

दानादाने यौतकस्य प्रकामं साधुगर्हिते ।
ददाति यदि चादत्ते तत्स्यात् सन्ततिविक्रयः ॥१८१ ॥

dānādāne yautakasya prakāmaṁ sādhugarhite ।
dadāti yadi cādatte tat syāt santativikrayaḥ ॥181 ॥

Both offering and accepting dowry as you like has always been despised by the noble-minded. Giving or receiving dowry, in effect, is equal to selling one's own children. [181]

कस्मैचिद्वचसा दत्तां नान्यस्मै वितरेद् वधूम् ।
व्यतिक्रमे धर्मभङ्गः तेन दुर्गतिमाप्नुयात् ॥१८२ ॥

kasmaicid vacasā dattāṁ nānyasmai vitared vadhūm ।
vyatikrame dharmabhaṅgaḥ tena durgatim āpnuyāt ॥182 ॥

A bride agreed to be given in marriage to a particular bridegroom should never be given to someone else. By disregarding this rule, one disrupts *dharma*, and it leads to misfortunes. [182]

कुष्ठक्षयश्वासकासहृद्रोगैर्निःस्वतादिभिः ।
पीडिता नैव कुर्वीरन् उद्वाहं तु कदाचन ॥१८३ ॥

kuṣṭha-kṣaya-śvāsakāsa-hṛdrogair niḥsvatādibhiḥ ।
pīḍitā naiva kurvīran udvāhaṁ tu kadācana ॥183 ॥

Those who are distressed with chronic diseases like leprosy, tuberculosis, breathing troubles, asthma, heart-disease and extreme poverty, should never get married. [183]

दंपत्योरथ कस्यापि रोगःसांक्रमिको यदि ।
त्याज्या निधुवनाकांक्षा लोकक्षेमचिकीर्षया ॥१८४ ॥

daṁpatyor atha kasyāpi rogaḥ sāṁkramiko yadi ।
tyājyā nidhuvanākāṅkṣā lokakṣema cikīrṣayā ॥184 ॥

If any of the couple, after marriage, becomes plagued by any infectious disease, they should give up sexual union, considering the well-being of the world. [184]

पञ्चके द्वे धर्मशुद्ध्योरनुतिष्ठेत् सदा गृही ।
तथा पञ्चमहायज्ञान् अतर्कितफलावहान् ॥१८५ ॥

pañcake dve dharmaśuddhyor anutiṣṭhet sadā gṛhī ।
tathā pañcamahāyajñān atarkitaphalāvahān ॥185 ॥

A householder should strictly adhere to the fivefold *dharma*s and the fivefold *śuddhi*s (purities) (mentioned earlier). So too he should perform the five great sacrifices (*pañcamahāyajña*s) of undebatable benefits. [185]

अष्टमः सर्गः (Canto Eight)

पञ्चमहायज्ञाः
(Five Great Sacrifices)

ब्राह्मः पित्र्यस्तथा दैवस्ततो भौतिकमानुषौ ।
एते पञ्चमहायज्ञाः प्रोच्यन्ते नयकोविदैः ॥१८६ ॥

brāhmaḥ pitryas tathā daivas tato bhautika-mānuṣau ।
ete pañcamahāyajñāḥ procyante nayakovidaiḥ ॥186 ॥

Related to *Brahman* (the Absolute), related to the ancestors (*pitṛ*s), related to gods, related to living beings, related to human beings — these are the fivefold great sacrifices as declared by those who are skilled in policy-making. [186]

ब्राह्मे यज्ञो जपः पाठः पाठनं पितृसंज्ञितः ।
पितॄणां तर्पणं दैवे होमो देवप्रसादनः ॥१८७ ॥

brāhme yajño japaḥ pāṭhaḥ pāṭhanaṁ pitṛsaṁjñitaḥ ।
pitṝṇāṁ tarpaṇaṁ daive homo devaprasādanaḥ ॥187 ॥

The sacrifice related to *Brahman* (*brahma-yajña*) consists of repeating sacred formulas (*japa*), learning and teaching. Making offerings to the manes (*pitṛ*s or souls of the ancestors) forms the sacrifice related to the ancestors (*pitṛ-yajña*). And the one related to gods (*daiva-yajña*) is constituted of performing fire sacrifices meant for pleasing gods. [187]

भूतयज्ञस्तिरश्चां यदाहारादि समर्पणम् ।
मानुष्योऽतिथिवर्ण्यार्त्तभृत्यानामपि पूजनम् ॥१८८ ॥

bhūtayajñas tiraścāṁ yad āhārādi samarpaṇam ।
mānuṣyo 'tithi-varṇy-ārtta-bhṛtyānām api pūjanam ॥188 ॥

Offering food and the like to animals, birds, etc., is the sacrifice related to living beings (*bhūta-yajña*). Adoringly doing service to guests, *brahmacārins*, those who are in trouble, and one's own servants, makes the sacrifice related to humans (*mānuṣa-yajña*). [188]

पञ्चयज्ञानकुर्वाणो नूनं दुर्गतिमाप्नुयात् ।
यज्ञावशिष्टभोक्तारः स्पृश्यन्ते न हि पाप्मभिः ॥१८९ ॥

pañcayajñān akurvāṇo nūnaṁ durgatim āpnuyāt ।
yajñāvaśiṣṭa-bhoktāraḥ spṛśyante na hi pāpmabhiḥ ॥189 ॥

He who does not perform the fivefold sacrifice surely has to face misfortunes. On the other hand, those who enjoy sustaining on the remainder of sacrifices remain ever untouched by sins. [189]

दैवात् पितृभ्यश्चावाप्तादप्रदाय मनागपि ।
तेभ्यः स्वयं हि यो भुङ्क्ते सोऽयं नित्यपतारकः ॥१९० ॥

daivāt pitṛbhyaś cāvāptād apradāya manāg api ।
tebhyaḥ svayaṁ hi yo bhuṅkte so 'yaṁ nityapatārakaḥ ॥190 ॥

He who enjoys for himself whatever he happens to possess god-given or by ancestral right, without sharing at least a bit with the above-mentioned, is indeed a persistent cheat. [190]

अविच्छिन्नप्रेमभाजौ वतेते यत्र दंपती ।
सर्वकल्याणसंपन्नं कुलं तदतिपावनम् ॥१९१ ॥

avicchinnapremabhājau vatete yatra daṁpatī ।
sarvakalyāṇa-saṁpannaṁ kulaṁ tad atipāvanam ॥191 ॥

The family where the couple live always as the abode of unbroken mutual love, is ceaselessly favoured by all propitious things, and is to be considered highly holy. [191]

पितृदैवातिथीनां च ज्ञातेः स्वस्य कृतेऽपि च ।
यो धर्म क्रियते नित्यं धर्माणामुत्तमः स हि ॥१९२ ॥

pitṛdaivātithīnāṁ ca jñāteḥ svasya kṛte'pi ca ।
yo dharma kriyate nityaṁ dharmāṇām uttamaḥ sa hi ॥192 ॥

The *dharma* observed daily intended for the benefit of the ancestors, gods, guests, close relatives and for oneself, is indeed to be counted as the best of all *dharmas*. [192]

पापभीत्या पक्वमन्नं विभज्य गृहिणोऽश्नतः ।
कदाप्यपत्यविच्छेदो न जायते सुचेतसः ॥१९३ ॥

pāpabhītyā pakvam annaṁ vibhajya gṛhiṇo 'śnataḥ ।
kadāpy apatyavicchedo na jāyate sucetasaḥ ॥193 ॥

A virtuous householder who habitually eats cooked food by sharing it with others for fear of being a sinner, will never have to face the misfortune of his lineage becoming cut-off. [193]

गृहस्थो धीरधीः स्वस्य धर्मान्न प्रच्युतो यदि ।
तत्रैव निरतः सर्वयतीनां मुख्य एव सः ॥१९४ ॥

gṛhastho dhīrdhīḥ svasya dharmān na pracyuto yadi ।
tatraiva nirataḥ sarvayatīnāṁ mukhya eva saḥ ॥194 ॥

If a strong-willed householder stands firmly for *dharma* all through his life, then he is to be considered first among those who are of full restraint (*yatis*). [194]

इतरान् धर्ममार्गेण चालयन्नविकंपितः ।
स्वधर्ममाचरन्मर्त्यो व्रतिश्रेष्ठो निगद्यते ॥१९५ ॥

itarān dharmamārgeṇa cālayann avikaṁpitaḥ ।
svadharmam ācaran martyo vratiśreṣṭho nigadyate ॥195 ॥

He who makes others move along the path of *dharma*, and who walks so himself with firmness, is to be called a *vratiśreṣṭha* (best among the observers of religions vows). [195]

गार्हस्थ्यमुत्तमो धर्मो यदि सर्वोपकारकः ।
अपकारपरं तच्चेद् अधर्म इति कथ्यते ॥१९६ ॥

gārhasthyam uttamo dharmo yadi sarvopakārakaḥ ।
apakāraparaṁ tac ced adharma iti kathyate ॥196 ॥

Being a householder, if helpful to all, is the best of all *dharmas*. It is said to be *adharma* (unrighteous), if harmful. [196]

स्वधर्माननतिक्रम्य भुवि वर्तेत यो गृही ।
देवराजसमः प्रेम्णा स्तूयते सर्वदेहिभिः ॥१९७ ॥

svadharmān anatikramya bhuvi varteta yo gṛhī ।
devarājasamaḥ premṇā stūyate sarva-dehibhiḥ ॥197 ॥

A householder who lives in this world without transgressing his own duties (*svadharmas*) is equal to the king of gods. He is lovingly praised by all beings. [197]

श्रेयःप्रेयःप्रदो धर्मः स तु सर्वोत्तमो भुवि ।
ततो महत्तरः कः स्याद् विशेषो मर्त्यजन्मनि ॥१९८ ॥

śreyaḥ-preyaḥprado dharmaḥ sa tu sarvottamo bhuvi ।
tato mahattaraḥ kaḥ syād viśeṣo martyajanmani ॥198 ॥

Dharma ensures the attainment of higher values (*śreyas*) in life, as well as of the worldly values (*preyas*), and is considered the noblest in this world. Higher than that, what is there to have in human life? [198]

प्रथमं पुष्पिता नारी सुस्नाता सप्तमेऽहनि ।
पुण्याहं शुद्धिहोमं च कारयित्वा विशुध्यति ॥१९९ ॥

prathamaṁ puṣpitā nārī susnātā saptame 'hani ।
puṇyāhaṁ śuddhihomaṁ ca kārayitvā viśudhyati ॥199 ॥

The girl who menstruates for the first time becomes purified by bathing on the seventh day, followed by performing the purificatory fire-sacrifices and sprinkling consecrated water in the surroundings. [199]

ततो योषित् क्रमेणैव मासि मासि रजस्वला ।
चतुर्थे दिवसे स्नात्वा शुद्धा होमादिना भवेत् ॥२०० ॥

tato yoṣit krameṇaiva māsi māsi rajasvalā ।
caturthe divase snātvā śuddhā homādinā bhavet ॥200 ॥

The woman, then, when menstruating month after month, should become purified by bathing and performing fire-sacrifices and the like, on the fourth day. [200]

पुष्पवत्युपयोगार्थं यद्वितीर्णं गृहादिकम् ।
सर्वं तस्याः स्नानदिने मार्जयेच्च जलादिभिः ॥२०१ ॥

puṣpavaty-upayogārthaṁ yad vitīrṇaṁ gṛhādikam ।
sarvaṁ tasyāḥ snānadine mārjayec ca jalādibhiḥ ॥201 ॥

The room and all the utensils used by the woman in menstruation should be made pure by wiping and cleaning with water, the same day she bathes. [201]

ऋतुस्नानदिनादूर्ध्वं द्वादशाहनि योषितं ।
वरोऽभिगच्छेद्योगाय प्रेम्णा पर्वादि वर्जयन् ॥२०२ ॥

ṛtusnānadinād ūrdhvaṁ dvādaśāhani yoṣitaṁ ।
varo 'bhigacched yogāya premṇā parvādi varjayan ॥202 ॥

Up to the twelfth day of the woman taking her purificatory bath after menstruation, her husband can have loveful sexual union with her. Doing so is to be avoided on the *parva* days (the eighth and fourteenth days of the lunar fortnight, and the new moon and fullmoon days). [202]

दिनानि द्वादशैतानि गर्भाधानक्षमाणि यत् ।
तत्तदात्त्वे पुत्रकामी जायामृच्छतु नान्यदा ॥२०३ ॥

dināni dvādaśaitāni garbhādhānakṣamāṇi yat ।
tat tadāttve putrakāmī jāyām ṛcchatu nānyadā ॥203 ॥

These twelve days being fit for begetting offspring, he who is desirous of having children should have union with his wife only on these days, never at any other time. [203]

गर्भाधानात् समारभ्य पितरौ ब्रह्मचारिणौ ।
स्यातां शिशोः स्तन्यपाननिवृत्यन्तं यताशयौ ॥२०४ ॥

garbhādhānāt samārabhya pitarau brahmacāriṇau ।
syātāṁ śiśoḥ stanyapāna-nivṛtyantaṁ yatāśayau ॥204 ॥

The couple, with self-restraint, should remain *brahmacārins* (should abstain from sex-relationship), beginning from the time of impregnation till the end of the breast-feeding of the baby. [204]

व्यतियाने महान् व्याधिरल्पायुष्ट्वं बलक्षयः ।
मातुः शिशोश्च जायेत स्तन्यं च विकरोति यत् ॥२०५ ॥

vyatiyāne mahān vyādhir alpāyuṣṭvaṁ balakṣayaḥ ।
mātuḥ śiśoś ca jāyeta stanyaṁ ca vikaroti yat ॥205 ॥

Any deviation from this rule results in both the mother and child having severe diseases, shortening of their life-span, and weakening of their bodily strength. Above all, the breast- milk also becomes befouled. [205]

अन्तर्वत्नी पयस्यं यत् द्रव्यं नियतमाहरेत् ।
सत्कथाश्रवणेनापि तुष्ट्या कालं नयेत् सती ॥२०६ ॥

antarvatnī payasyaṁ yat dravyaṁ niyatam āharet ।
satkathāśravaṇenāpi tuṣṭyā kālaṁ nayet satī ॥206 ॥

A pregnant woman should eat nourishing food enriched with milk-content. She should remain happy listening to good stories of moral import. [206]

न केनापि प्रकारेण दुःखमेषा समश्नुयात् ।
असमञ्जसवृत्तानां चिन्तनं च विवर्जयेत् ॥२०७ ॥

na kenāpi prakāreṇa duḥkham eṣā samaśnuyāt ।
asamañjasavṛttānāṁ cintanaṁ ca vivarjayet ॥207 ॥

In no way she should be subjected to sufferings. Thinking of improper affairs also is to be given up by her. [207]

सर्वलक्षणसंपन्नं बुद्धिमन्तं गुणोत्तरम् ।
सुवै सुतं सुखमिति प्रार्थयेत् गर्भिणी स्वयम् ॥२०८ ॥

sarvalakṣaṇa-saṁpannaṁ buddhimantaṁ guṇottaram ।
suvai sutaṁ sukham iti prārthayet garbhiṇī svayam ॥208 ॥

The pregnant woman on her own should constantly pray, "May I give birth with ease to a child of all the signs of virtue, bright intelligence and good character." [208]

आगर्भगशिशोरन्त्यशय्याशयजनाद् गृही ।
जनस्योच्चावचस्यापि सेवने निरतो भवेत् ॥२०९ ॥

āgarbhagaśiśor antyaśayyāśayajanād gṛhī ।
janasyoccāvacasyāpi sevane nirato bhavet ॥209 ॥

A householder should diligently attend to the needs of everyone, of high position or low position, from the foetus lying in the womb to those who are on their death-beds. [209]

समुदायस्य राष्ट्रस्य धर्मस्यार्थस्य वा कृते ।
कृतिनः प्रयतन्ते ते गृहिणो मतिशालिनः ॥२१० ॥

samudāyasya rāṣṭrasya dharmasyārthasya vā kṛte ।
kṛtinaḥ prayatante te gṛhiṇo matiśālinaḥ ॥210 ॥

Noble-minded and skilful householders constantly make efforts for the betterment of the society, state, *dharma* (righteousness) and *artha* (worldly wealth). [210]

ब्रह्मचर्यं च संन्यासं श्रद्धावद्पर्यवेक्षणे ।
गृहस्थस्यावतिष्ठेते भूयः श्रेयस्करावुभौ ॥२११ ॥

brahmacaryaṁ ca saṁnyāsaṁ śraddhāvad paryavekṣaṇe ।
gṛhasthasyāvatiṣṭhete bhūyaḥ śreyaskarāvubhau ॥211 ॥

To the householder who takes care of the well-being of *brahmacārins* and *saṁnyāsins* with all faith, both become causal to attaining higher values in life. [211]

राजाधिकारो धर्मश्च लोकसंस्थितिरेव च ।
पौरे गृहिणि वर्तन्ते सर्वाधारस्ततो गृही ॥२१२ ॥

rājādhikāro dharmaś ca lokasaṁsthitir eva ca ।
paure gṛhiṇi vartante sarvādhāras tato gṛhī ॥212 ॥

The authority of the king or of the government, *dharma*s, the well-being of the world — all these base themselves on the householder-citizens. Therefore, householders form the firm support of everything. [212]

अतः सर्वेष्वाश्रमेषु गार्हस्थ्यं तदनुत्तमम् ।
इति सर्वे प्रशंसन्ति विद्वांसस्तत्त्वदर्शिनः ॥२१३ ॥

ataḥ sarveṣvāśrameṣu gārhasthyaṁ tad anuttamam ।
iti sarve praśaṁsanti vidvāṁsas tattvadarśinaḥ ॥213 ॥

Therefore, none of the *āśrama*s is superior to the householder's, as is hailed by all the learned seers of Reality. [213]

गृहस्थाश्रमधर्मान् या जनता ह्यवमन्यते ।
तस्या गच्छत्यधो भूतिः प्रभावोऽभ्युदयोऽपि च ॥२१४ ॥

gṛhasthāśrama-dharmān yā janatā hy avamanyate ।
tasyā gacchatyadho bhūtiḥ prabhāvo 'bhyudayo 'pi ca ॥214 ॥

The prosperity, splendour and success of the people who belittle the righteous duties of householders, meet with downfall. [214]

इति सम्यग्विमृश्यैतन्निर्वाह्यमिति चेन्मतिः ।
प्रसन्ना स्यात्ततः प्राज्ञो गार्हस्थ्याय प्रवर्तताम् ॥२१५ ॥

iti samyag vimṛśyaitan nirvāhyam iti cen matiḥ ।
prasannā syāt tataḥ prājño gārhasthyāya pravartatām ॥215 ॥

If one, having become fully aware of the nature of householder's life being so, after reflecting on it well and then decides with a pleasant mind, "I should take to it," then let that wise one make efforts for leading a householder's life. [215]

आश्रित्यानवधानेन गार्हस्थ्यं तु महत्तरम् ।
तन्निकृष्टतरं कुर्वन् लोकानर्थाय जीवति ॥२१६ ॥

āśrityānavadhānena gārhasthyaṁ tu mahattaram ।
tan nikr̥ṣṭataraṁ kurvan lokānarthāya jīvati ॥216 ॥

One who, without being mindful of the greatness of a householder's life, undergoes it in a despicable way, in effect, harms the world. [216]

सुबहुत्वे तादृशानां अविचार्यकृतामिह ।
नश्येयुराश्रमाः सर्वे लोकस्यापि क्षयो भवेत् ॥२१७ ॥

subahutve tādr̥śānāṁ avicāryakr̥tām iha ।
naśyeyur āśramāḥ sarve lokasyāpi kṣayo bhavet ॥217 ॥

The increase in number of such people who thoughtlessly get engaged in (householders') activities, results in the downfall of all the *āśrama*s. It causes even the decline of the world order. [217]

विवाहस्तु विनोदाय परमैहिकजीविते ।
सुखायेदं हितं किञ्चित् कर्मेति च न चिन्तयेत् ॥२१८ ॥

vivāhastū vinodāya paramaihikajīvite ।
sukhāyedaṁ hitaṁ kiñcit karmeti ca na cintayet ॥218 ॥

No one should ever think that marriage is meant for pleasure in this life, and that pleasure-seeking is the sole goal of useful activities. [218]

तद्गार्हस्थ्यप्रवेशार्थी श्रद्दधानो हि निर्भरम् ।
सुविचिन्त्य विवाहं तं विदधीत यथाक्रमम् ॥२१९ ॥

tad gārhasthya-praveśārthī śraddadhāno hi nirbharam ।
suvicintya vivāhaṁ taṁ vidadhīta yathākramam ॥219 ॥

Therefore the one who wishes to enter the householder's life should do so with complete faith in it, and should get married thoughtfully in the proper way. [219]

विद्यावित्तवयोरूपशीलाद्येष्वानुरूप्यतः ।
मिथोऽनुरागो दांपत्यस्थित्यै सुदृढशृङ्खला ॥२२० ॥

vidyāvittavayorūpa-śīlādyeṣvānurūpyataḥ ।
mitho'nurāgo dāṁpatyasthityai sudṛḍhaśṛṅkhalā ॥220 ॥

The mutual love between the couple ensured by matching in respect of their education, wealth, age, bodily beauty and habits, is the strong chain that helps their married life remain inflexible. [220]

जननं सकृदेव स्यान्मनुष्यस्य मृतिः सकृत् ।
असकृज्जायते भूमावनवस्थितजीवनः ॥२२१ ॥

jananaṁ sakṛd eva syān manuṣyasya mṛtiḥ sakṛt ।
asakṛj jāyate bhūmāvanavasthitajīvanaḥ ॥221 ॥

असकन् म्रियते भीरुः तथा चपलमानसः ।
एतावुभौ विवाहार्हौ न भवेतां कदाचन ॥२२२ ॥

asakṛn mriyate bhīruḥ tathā capalamānasaḥ ।
etāvubhau vivāhārhau na bhavetāṁ kadācana ॥222 ॥

Man normally is born only once; so too he dies only once. But those who live in this world systemless, take birth more than once. So too fickle-minded cowardly persons die more than once. These two kinds of people (those who live systemless and those who are fickle-minded and cowardly), in no case are fit for marrying. [221-222]

अनुरागो मनुष्यस्य स्यादेकत्रैव सुस्थिरः ।
ततः पुमानेकदैव कुर्याद् वैवाहिकं विधिम् ॥२२३ ॥

anurāgo manuṣyasya syād ekatraiva susthiraḥ ।
tataḥ pumān ekadaiva kuryād vaivāhikaṁ vidhim ॥223 ॥

Conjugal love remaining constant with one person is normal to human nature. Therefore, marrying is to be done by humans only once in life. [223]

शिष्या ऊचुः —

अकालिकी यदि मृतिर्भवेद्वध्वा वरस्य वा ।
अवशिष्टो जनः पश्चाद् उद्वहेद्वा न वानघ ॥२२४ ॥

akālikī yadi mṛtir bhaved vadhvā varasya vā ।
avaśiṣṭo janaḥ paścād udvahed vā na vānagha ॥224 ॥

The disciples said:

O the sinless one, if the wife or husband happens to die untimely, should the remaining one get married or not? [224]

गुरुरुवाच —

आस्था गृहव्रते भूयो यौवनौजश्च चेद्ध्रुवम् ।
आयुष्मान् पुनरुद्वाहं कुर्यात् साधुविचिन्तयन् ॥२२५ ॥

āsthā gṛhavrate bhūyo yauvanaujaś ca ced dhruvam ।
āyuṣmān punar udvāhaṁ kuryāt sādhu-vicintayan ॥225 ॥

In case the desire for married life as well as youthful vigour continues to exist in the person concerned, he or she of long life can remarry after giving due consideration to it. [225]

पुनर्विवाहस्तु सकृद् विधातव्यो न चासकृत् ।
अनेकवारं विहितः पुण्योच्छेदाय कल्पते ॥२२६ ॥

punar vivāhastu sakṛd vidhātavyo na cāsakṛt ।
anekavāraṁ vihitaḥ puṇyocchedāya kalpate ॥226 ॥

Remarrying, if at all, should be done once only. It should never be done more than once. Marrying many times results in the extinction of merits (*puṇya*). [226]

आरोग्यमनुरागश्च समप्राधान्यमर्हतः ।
तस्मादुत्पत्तिपत्रस्य दंपत्योः शोधनादपि ॥२२७ ॥

ārogyam anurāgaś ca samaprādhānyam arhataḥ ।
tasmād utpattipatrasya daṁpatyoḥ śodhanād api ॥227 ॥

कारयेद्भिषजा सम्यक् तदारोग्यपरीक्षणम् ।
पुनर्विवाहवैरल्यमाधातुमुपयोगिनाम् ॥२२८ ॥

kārayed bhiṣajā samyak tad ārogyaparīkṣaṇam ।
punarvivāhavairalyam ādhātum upayoginām ॥228 ॥

Health and mutual love are equally important (in married iife). Therefore, the healthiness of the couple is to be ensured even by undergoing medical tests of the genitals. This becomes a necessity in order to reduce the occasion for remarrying. [227-228]

अरोगिणामपत्यानां लाभायैनं प्रशस्यते ।
श्वशुरौ नवदंपत्योः गृहधर्मोपदेशकौ ॥२२९ ॥

aroginām apatyānāṁ lābhāyainaṁ praśasyate ।
śvaśurau navadaṁpatyoḥ gṛhadharmopadeśakau ॥229 ॥

This system is commendable as it ensures healthy progeny. The parents of the newly married couple should instruct them on the proper duties of a householder. [229]

सस्नेहमनुवर्तेरन् गुरवो नवदंपती ।
स्वातन्त्र्यमपबाध्यैव रुद्धन्त्वनयमेतयोः ॥२३० ॥

sasneham anuvarteran guravo navadaṁpatī ।
svātantryam apabādhyaiva ruddhantv anayam etayoḥ ॥230 ॥

Seniors of the family should behave with the newly weds with affection. Their misbehaviours should be stopped without curbing their sense of freedom. [230]

अन्योन्यक्लेशकारिण्योः स्नुषाश्वश्रोर्निकेतनम् ।
अनेकविभवोपेतमपि देवः परित्यजेत् ॥२३१ ॥

anyonyakleśakāriṇyoḥ snuṣāśvaśror niketanam ।
anekavibhavopetam api devaḥ parityajet ॥231 ॥

The household in which the daughter-in-law and the father-in-law (or the mother-in-law) are in constant quarrel, should be left by the husband even if prosperous in other respects. [231]

भार्यामुद्वेजयन् भर्ता क्रीतभृत्यो भयप्रभुः ।
अनुरागस्तत्र तस्याः स्थिरतामुपयाति चेत् ॥२३२ ॥

bhāryām udvejayan bhartā krītabhṛtyo bhayaprabhuḥ ।
anurāgastatra tasyāḥ sthiratām upayāti cet ॥232 ॥

साश्चर्यं तादृशीं शान्तां आराधयति देवता ।
नृशंसं निर्दयं तं तु द्वेष्टि चान्ते शपत्यपि ॥२३३ ॥

sāścaryaṁ tādṛśīṁ śāntāṁ ārādhayati devatā ।
nṛśaṁsaṁ nirdyaṁ taṁ tu dveṣṭi cānte śapaty api ॥233 ॥

Even when constantly troubled by her husband by buying a servant or having become frightened, if the wife maintains well-stabilized love towards that husband, then that woman wonderfully will be worshipped by God. And more, God will hate that cruel and troublemaker-husband, and finally will curse him. [232-233]

दंपत्योः समभागित्वं सुखे दुःखे च सङ्गते ।
सहकारित्वमनघं कृत्यनिर्वहणे मिथः ॥२३४ ॥

daṁpatyoḥ samabhāgitvaṁ sukhe duḥkhe ca saṅgate ।
sahakāritvam anaghaṁ kṛtyanirvahaṇe mithaḥ: ॥234 ॥

The couple should share with each other all the relevant matters both in happiness and suffering. There should also be harmless co-operation between each other in all the household affairs. [234]

प्रेमविस्रंभविध्वंसिमार्गे नित्याप्रवर्तनम् ।
अन्योन्यागः प्रकाश्यैतच्छोधनं धर्मलक्षणम् ॥२३५ ॥

premavisraṁbhavidhvaṁsimārge nityāpravartanam ।
anyonyāgaḥ prakāśyaitacchodhanaṁ dharmalakṣaṇam ॥235 ॥

They should always keep themselves away from activities detrimental to their mutual love and trust. The best sign of good householders is the couple pointing out to one another what is defective in each, and thus correcting such faults. [235]

कमितुः कुलसंस्थाया अनुरोधिगुणालया ।
आयानुकूलव्ययवत्यमला गृहिणी मता ॥२३६ ॥

kaṃituḥ kulasaṁsthāyā anurodhiguṇālayā ।
āyānukūlavyayavaty amalā gṛhiṇī matā ॥236 ॥

A woman who is well-bred, having qualities that find harmony with those of the husband, innocent, and who spends in accordance with the household income, is the best mistress of a house. [236]

कुटुंबिनी गुणापेता यदि सर्वोत्तमं कुलम् ।
गुणहीनं भवेन्नूनं क्रमशो नाशमश्नुयात् ॥२३७ ॥

kuṭuṁbinī guṇāpetā yadi sarvottamaṁ kulam ।
guṇahīnaṁ bhaven nūnaṁ kramaśo nāśam aśnuyāt ॥237 ॥

Even the best of all families, if the mistress of the house is qualityless, becomes equally qualityless, and, in course of time, decays. [237]

यदि सा स्याद् गुणवती दुरवस्थासमाकुलं ।
कुटुंबमपि कालेन वर्धेत सगुणं शनैः ॥२३८ ॥

yadi sā syād guṇavatī duravasthāsamākulaṁ ।
kuṭuṁbam api kālena vardheta saguṇaṁ śanaiḥ ॥238 ॥

If the mistress of the house is of good qualities, then even the family life that is full of distresses, gradually attains a better state. [238]

आर्जनीयपदार्थानां मनुष्यस्योत्तमोत्तमम् ।
द्रव्यं कलत्रमेव स्यात् चारित्रगुणभूषितम् ॥२३९ ॥

ārjanīyapadārthānāṁ manuṣyottamottamam ।
dravyaṁ kalatrameva syāt cāritraguṇabhūṣitam ॥239 ॥

The best among the best of treasures one can have in life, is a wife adorned with ideal character. [239]

आत्मानं पालितवती शुश्रूषन्ती स्वनायकम् ।
यशोभङ्गमकुर्वन्ती वर्तमानोत्तमा सती ॥२४० ॥

ātmānaṁ pālitavatī śuśrūṣantī svanāyakam ।
yaśobhaṅgam akurvantī vartamānottamā satī ॥240 ॥

She who lives looking after herself, who takes care of her husband well, who does not become involved in reproachable activities, is the best mistress of a house. [240]

अन्तःपुरमहाकारां हित्वाऽपि स्वयमेव या ।
गोपायति स्वचारित्रं एषा स्याद्दयितोत्तमा ॥२४१ ॥

antaḥpura-mahākārāṁ hitvā 'pi svayam eva yā ।
gopāyati svacāritraṁ eṣā syād dayitottamā ॥241 ॥

She who takes care of the purity of her character even at the cost of leaving her own chambers, is the best among women. [241]

वात्यायामचलो दीपो लक्ष्मी सर्वार्थरूपिणी ।
चारुसौशील्यनिलया महती गृहनायिका ॥२४२ ॥

vātyāyām acalo dīpo lakṣmī sarvārtharūpiṇī ।
cārusauśīlyanilayā mahatī gṛhanāyikā ॥242 ॥

She who remains like a lamp-flame unflickering even in high winds, who shines like Lakṣmī, the embodiment of all wealth, who is the abode of ideal and gentle character, is the greatest house-mistress. [242]

एतादृशो समं भर्ता तत्तद्धर्मान्निरन्तरम् ।
कुर्वन्नेवेह गार्हस्थ्यं अविघ्नं परिपालयेत् ॥२४३ ॥

etādṛśo samaṁ bhartā tat tad dharmān nirantaram ।
kurvann eveha gārhasthyaṁ avighnaṁ paripālayet ॥243 ॥

Along with such a wife, a husband should discharge his duties of a householder obstructionless, by doing the proper things intended to be done by him, constantly as and when such become necessary. [243]

अनन्तकल्याणनिधानमेतद्
गार्हस्थ्यमाशास्यममायमेवम् ।
समाचरन् वाञ्छितमेत्य सर्वं
निरन्तरानन्दपदं प्रयाति ॥२४४ ॥

anantakalyāṇa-nidhānam etad
gārhasthyam āśāsyam amāyam evam ।
samācaran vāñchitam etya sarvaṁ
nirantarānanda-padaṁ prayāti ॥244 ॥

The one who undergoes this householder's state of life (*gārhasthya*), the repository of infinite auspicious things, in a commendable and unadulterated manner, fulfils all the desires in life, and attains the blissful state of enjoying unbroken contentment. [244]

नवमः सर्गः (Canto Nine)

अपरक्रियाः
(Funeral Rites)

शिष्या ऊचुः —

करुणारसकल्लोलमालान्तःस्थितमानस ।
संशीतिरपरा काचिद् अस्माकं भवति प्रभो ॥२४५ ॥

karuṇārasakallola-mālāntaḥ-sthitamānasa ।
saṁśītiraparā kācid asmākaṁ bhavati prabho ॥285 ॥

The disciples said:

O Lord whose mind is filled with the rows of uprising waves of the essence of kindness, we have yet another doubt to be cleared now. [245]

केनापि हेतुना मर्त्यो मृत्युमाप्नोत्यसंशयम् ।
प्रेतस्य किं वा कर्तव्यं इत्युक्त्वा तामपाकुरु ॥२४६ ॥

kenāpi hetunā martyo mṛtyum āpnoty asaṁśayam ।
pretasya kiṁ vā kartavyaṁ ity uktvā tām apākuru ॥246 ॥

Man, for one reason or another, doubtlessly will attain death. Kindly clear our above-mentioned doubt as to what to do with the dead body. [246]

गुरुरुवाच —

निशम्यानुक्रमात् पृच्छां युष्माकमुपयोगिनीम् ।
सम्यङ्मोदेन वक्ष्यामि संक्षेपादपरक्रियाम् ॥२४७ ॥

niśamyānukramāt pṛcchāṁ yuṣmākam upayoginīm ।
samyaṅ modena vakṣyāmi saṁkṣepād aparakriyām ॥247 ॥

The Guru said:

As asked by you in an orderly manner, I shall happily tell you properly and summarily about the funeral rites, always beneficial to you. [247]

स्त्रीबालयुववृद्धानां मरणे सति तच्छवान् ।
प्रदहेत् परितः शुद्ध्यै नान्यथा विधिरिष्यते ॥२४८ ॥

strībālayuvavṛddhānāṁ maraṇe sati tacchavān ।
pradahet paritaḥ śuddhyai nānyathā vidhir iṣyate ॥248 ॥

Whether a woman, child, youth or an old-aged person, when dead, the dead body should be cremated in order to ensure purity of the environment. No other rule is there on this matter. [248]

शवाशौचो दशाहानि ज्ञातीनामिह निश्चितः ।
एकादशे दिने कुर्यात् होमं पुण्याहमेव च ॥२४९ ॥

śavāśauco daśāhāni jñātīnām iha niścitaḥ ।
ekādaśe dine kuryāt homaṁ puṇyāham eva ca ॥249 ॥

Defilement caused by the death is decided to be observed for ten days by close relatives. Performing fire sacrifice and sprinkling consecrated water should be done on the eleventh day. [249]

तदन्ते विधिवत्स्नानात् शुद्धिर्जायेत तद्दिने ।
ततः परं न कर्त्तव्यः प्रेतोद्देश्यो विधिः क्वचित् ॥२५० ॥

tad ante vidhivat snānāt śuddhir jāyeta tad dine ।
tataḥ paraṁ na karttavyaḥ pretoddeśyo vidhiḥ kvacit ॥250 ॥

At the end of these rites should be performed the formal bathing as is prescribed. With these observances purity is regained the very same day. [250]

पितुः पिण्डप्रदः पुत्रः पौत्रो वा तदभावतः ।
तस्याप्यभावे सोदर्यः तत्पुत्रो वा नियम्यताम् ॥२५१ ॥

pituḥ piṇḍapradaḥ putraḥ pautro vā tad abhāvataḥ ।
tasyāpyabhāve sodaryaḥ tat putro vā niyamyatām ॥251 ॥

The last rite of offering rice-ball (*piṇḍa*) is to be done by the son. In his absence it could be done by the grandson. In case a grandson is also absent, the son of a brother could be deputed for this purpose. [251]

प्रस्तुतानामसत्वे तु भागिनेयोऽपि सम्मतः ।
यद्वा पिण्डप्रदातृत्वं दंपत्योः स्यात् परस्परम् ॥२५२ ॥

prastutānām asatve tu bhāgineyo 'pi sammataḥ ।
yadvā piṇḍapradātṛtvaṁ daṁpatyoḥ syāt parasparam ॥252 ॥

In the absence of any of the above, the nephew (sister's son) doing it is also acceptable. Or else, the right for doing the offering of *piṇḍa* could be between each other in the case of a couple. [252]

परेतस्य विधिः सर्वोप्याशौचादिर्निरर्थकः ।
अज्ञातायाः विलासः स्यादिति यस्य मनःस्थितिः ॥२५३ ॥

paretasya vidhiḥ sarvopyāśaucādir nirarthakaḥ ।
ajñatāyāḥ vilāsaḥ syād iti yasya manaḥsthitiḥ ॥253 ॥

निर्विकल्पस्य तस्यायं विधिः कार्यो न जात्वपि ।
अनीदृशस्य सर्वस्य विधिरेष नियम्यते ॥२५४ ॥

nirvikalpasya tasyāyaṁ vidhiḥ kāryo na jātvapi ।
anīdṛśasya sarvasya vidhir eṣa niyamyate ॥254 ॥

Such precepts are not at all to be complied with in the case of those who are fully convinced that the observance of defilement and all the connected purificatory rites are meaningless, and that such are only signs of ignorance proliferating. These precepts are meant for all others only. [253-254]

स तु तत्तत्कालदेशानुकूलश्च निरुह्यतां ।
पुरोहितनियुक्तेन वर्त्मना कर्मतत्परैः ॥२५५ ॥

sa tu tat tat kāladeśānukūlaś ca niruhyatāṁ ।
purohitaniyuktena vartmanā karmatatparaiḥ ॥255 ॥

Let these precepts be practised by those who are interested in rituals, as directed by priests, making due allowance for spatial and temporal contingencies. [255]

दशमः सर्गः (Canto Ten)

संन्यासः
(Renunciation or *Saṁnyāsa*)

शिष्या ऊचुः —

भगवन् करुणामूर्त्ते तत्त्वलक्ष्यप्रकाशक ।
अद्वैततत्त्ववेत्तॄणां प्रवरानन्दशेवधे ॥२५६ ॥

bhagavan karuṇāmūrtte tattvalakṣyaprakāśaka ।
advaitatattvavettṝṇāṁ pravarānandaśevadhe ॥256 ॥

भवता प्रेतसंस्कारस्तदाशौचश्च तद्विधिः ।
उपदिष्टश्च विधिवत् श्रुतोऽस्माभिः समाहितैः ॥२५७ ॥

bhavatā pretasaṁskāras tadāśaucaśca tad vidhiḥ ।
upadiṣṭaś ca vidhivat śruto 'smābhiḥ samāhitaiḥ ॥257 ॥

The disciples said:

O the embodiment of compassion, O the revealer of the ultimate Goal and Reality, O the best among the knowers of the secret of non-dual Reality, O the abode of ultimate Bliss! [256]

We have attentively heard from you the precepts on how to properly dispose of a dead body, and how to perform the related purificatory rites. [257]

संन्यासाश्रमधर्मश्च श्रोतुमीहामहे वयम् ।
तदपि ब्रूहि तत्त्वज्ञ नित्यनिर्वाणकारणम् ॥२५८ ॥

saṁnyāsāśramadharmaś ca śrotum īhāmahe vayam ।
tad api brūhi tattvajña nityanirvāṇakāraṇam ॥258 ॥

We are eager to hear from you about the *dharma* of *saṁnyāsa-āāśrama* also. O knower of the ultimate Reality, kindly expound to us that *dharma* also, which really leads one to eternal *nirvāṇa* (final absorption). [258]

गुरुरुवाचः —

शैशवाद् ब्रह्मचर्यञ्च तस्माद् गार्हस्थ्यमेत्य च ।
तदाश्रमीयधर्मैर्यः शान्तोऽन्ते संन्यसेत् पुमान् ॥२५९ ॥

śaiśavād brahmacaryañ ca tasmād gārhasthyam etya ca ।
tad āśramīyadharmairyaḥ śānto 'nte saṁnyaset pumān ॥259 ॥

Having reached *brahmacarya* from infancy, and after having reached the householder's state from *brahmacarya*, one, on becoming free from passions by performing the duties related to these *āśrama*s in their order, should take to the *saṁnyāsa-āāśrama*. [259]

शान्तादिसाधनवती नित्यानित्यविवेकिनी ।
विरक्तिभरिता योषित् पुंवत्संन्यासमर्हति ॥२६० ॥

śāntādi sādhanavatī nityānityavivekinī ।
viraktibharitā yoṣit puṁvatsaṁnyāsam arhati ॥260 ॥

A woman, who has practised such spiritual disciplines as *śama* (self-restraint), who is capable of discriminating the eternal from the transient, who has become fully detached from worldly values, is competent to take to *saṁnyāsa*, like a man of the same qualities. [260]

वर्णी गृही वा वैराग्यात् संन्यस्तुं यदपेक्षते ।
कालानपेक्षमाचार्यः तदा संन्यासयेदमुम् ॥२६१ ॥

varṇī gṛhī vā vairāgyāt saṁnyastuṁ yad apekṣate ।
kālānapekṣam ācāryaḥ tadā saṁnyāsayed amum ॥261 ॥

If a *brahmacārin* or householder, on becoming fully convinced of having attained complete detachment, applies for *saṁnyāsa*, then the *guru* should initiate him or her into *saṁnyāsa*, irrespective of his or her age. [261]

आचार्यस्यानुमतिं अनवाप्य स्वमेधया ।
न संन्यसेदक्षमया कोऽपि विक्षिप्तमानसः ॥२६२ ॥

ācāryasyānumatiṁ anavāpya svamedhayā ।
na saṁnyased akṣamayā ko 'pi vikṣiptamānasaḥ ॥262 ॥

Without getting the permission of the *guru*, no one, in a confused state of mind, should take *saṁnyāsa* impatiently on his own. [262]

वैराग्यचित्तवैशद्यविवेकरहितः पुमान् ।
अर्हत्येव न संन्यासं भृष्टं बीजमिवाङ्कुरम् ॥२६३ ॥

vairāgya-cittavaiśadya-vivekarahitaḥ pumān ।
arhatyeva na saṁnyāsaṁ bhr̥ṣṭaṁ bījam ivāṅkuram ॥262 ॥

In one who lacks a sense of detachment, clarity of mind and discrimination, *saṁnyāsa* will not sprout, as in the case of a roasted seed. [263]

स्वमित्रेषु कुटुंबे वा माऽस्तु स्नेहः परं यतेः ।
समजीविषु यः स्नेहः स तत्रापि प्रशस्यते ॥२६४ ॥

svamitreṣu kuṭuṁbe vā mā 'stu snehaḥ paraṁ yateḥ ।
samajīviṣu yaḥ snehaḥ sa tatrāpi praśasyate ॥264 ॥

A *saṁnyāsin* should not love his family members and friends excessively. The love he has for every being, being shown equally to them also is commendable. [264]

न स्निह्येत् केवलं किञ्चित् शुद्धान्तःकरणो यतिः ।
लोकेऽस्मिन् प्राणिनः सर्वे परिव्राजः सहोदराः ॥२६५ ॥

na snihyet kevalaṁ kiñcit śuddhāntaḥkaraṇo yatiḥ ।
loke 'smin prāṇinaḥ sarve parivrājaḥ sahodarāḥ ॥265 ॥

Loving something particularly does not become a *saṁnyāsin*'s habit. All living beings in this world are brothers for a *saṁnyāsin*. [265]

आचार्यानुज्ञया पूर्वं पुमान् मुण्डितमस्तकः ।
विरजाहोमो परमः समेत्य गुरुसन्निधिम् ॥२६६ ॥

ācāryānujñayā pūrvaṁ pumān muṇḍitamastakaḥ ।
virajāhomo paramaḥ sametya gurusannidhim ॥266 ॥

प्रदक्षणीकृत्य गुरुं साष्टाङ्गप्रणतोत्थितः ।
काषायवसनं तस्माद् आददीत कमण्डलुम् ॥२६७ ॥

pradakṣaṇīkṛtya guruṁ sāṣṭāṅgapraṇatotthitaḥ ।
kāṣāyavasanaṁ tasmād ādadīta kamaṇḍalum ॥267 ॥

First one should get the permission of the *guru*, and then should become shaven-headed. After having performed the *virajā homa* (burnt sacrifice symbolizing one's withdrawal from all worldly matters), one should present oneself before the *guru*. [266]

After formally circumambulating the *guru* clockwise, and after prostrating before the *guru* in salutation, one should accept the ochre-cloth and water-pot (*kamaṇḍalu*) from the *guru*. [267]

जपध्यानोपासनानि शौचं च प्राणसंयमम् ।
गुरूपदिष्टमार्गेण चरेन्नित्यं यतेन्द्रियः ॥२६८ ॥

japadhyānopāsanāni śaucaṁ ca prāṇasaṁyamam ।
gurūpadiṣṭamārgeṇa caren nityaṁ yatendriyaḥ ॥268 ॥

A *saṁnyāsin*, with restrained sense-organs, should practise muttering of incantations, meditation and adoration, along with cleanliness and breath-control, as instructed by the *guru*. [268]

प्राणमुक्तं यतेर्देहं दाहयेन्न कदाचन ।
खनित्वा विधिवत्भूमिं स्थापयित्वोपरिप्रियं ॥२६९ ॥

prāṇamuktaṁ yater dehaṁ dāhayen na kadācana ।
khanitvā vidhivat bhūmiṁ sthāpayitvoparipriyaṁ ॥269 ॥

अश्वत्थबिल्वचूतादि द्रुणामन्यतमं क्षिपेत् ।
अशौचादि विधानं स्यात् न कस्यापि मृते यतौ ॥२७० ॥

aśvattha bilva cūtādi druṇām anyatamaṁ kṣipet ।
aśaucādi vidhānaṁ syāt na kasyāpi mṛte yatau ॥270 ॥

The dead body of a *saṁnyāsin* should never be cremated. It should be let go into a hole made in the earth in conformity to customs. [269]

And over it is to be planted one of the trees such as fig., *bilva* (wood-apple), mango, etc. liked by him. No impurity related to the death of a *saṁnyāsin* occurs to anyone. [270]

मठं देवालयं वापि जनतामन्दिरं गुहाम् ।
नद्यास्तीरञ्च सामुद्रं ब्रह्मचारीनिकेतनम् ॥२७१ ॥

maṭhaṁ devālayaṁ vāpi janatāmandiraṁ guhām ।
nadyāstīrañca sāmudraṁ brahmacārīniketanam ॥271 ॥

निवासायाश्रयेत्कामं संन्यासी यतमानसः ।
अन्यत्र न वसेद्गेहे स्वधर्मापायकारणात् ॥२७२ ॥

nivāsāyāśrayet kāmaṁ saṁnyāsī yatamānasaḥ ।
anyatra na vased gehe svadharmāpāyakāraṇāt ॥272 ॥

A *muṭha* (monastery), temple, way-side inn, cave, river-bank, sea-coast, or a *brahmacārin*'s residence, as he likes, could be made use of by a *saṁnyāsin* of self-restraint, for his abode. He should reside in no other household; doing so is likely to endanger his natural way of living. [271-272]

दुर्निवारापदि प्राज्ञो गृहस्थस्य गृहे वसेत् ।
दिनानि त्रीणि संन्यासी तत ऊर्ध्वं न किञ्चन ॥२७३ ॥

durnivārāpadi prājño gṛhasthasya gṛhe vaset ।
dināni trīṇi saṁnyāsī tata ūdhvaṁ na kiñcana ॥273 ॥

An enlightened *saṁnyāsin*, in unavoidable adverse circumstances, could stay in the residence of a householder, for three days. In no case should the stay be prolonged. [273]

सङ्घं भजेयुर्यतीनां यतयो वीतकल्मषाः ।
समानधर्मसंबन्धः सर्वेषां श्रेयसे भवेत् ॥२७४ ॥

saṁghaṁ bhajeyur yatīnāṁ yatayo vītakalmaṣāḥ ।
samānadharma-saṁbandhaḥ sarveṣāṁ śreyase bhavet ॥274 ॥

Saṁnyāsins of purified mind may form an association (*saṁgha*) of themselves. Being based on common higher values, such an association will lead everyone to a blessed state. [274]

मोक्षार्थमुत्तमो धर्मो ज्ञानसंपादनं यतेः ।
समाधिश्च गुरुप्रोक्तवर्त्मना सिद्धिमिच्छतः ॥२७५ ॥

mokṣārtham uttamo dharmo jñānasaṁpādanaṁ yateḥ ।
samādhiś ca guruprokta-vartmanā siddhim icchataḥ ॥274 ॥

The best and righteous means, as far as a *saṁnyāsin* is concerned, for realizing *mokṣa* (final liberation), is attaining wisdom. The one who yearns for the final attainment experiences *samādhi* by treading the path taught by the *guru*. [275]

लोके परोपकारार्थं कर्म कुर्याद् गतस्पृहः ।
तेन चित्तप्रसादः स्याद् ज्ञानं च क्रमशो यतेः ॥२७६ ॥

loke paropakārārthaṁ karma kuryād gataspṛhaḥ ।
tena cittaprasādaḥ syād jñānaṁ ca kramaśo yateḥ ॥276 ॥

Motivated by no desires, a *saṁnyāsin* in this world should remain engaged in activities for the benefit of others. This eventually leads one to full blessedness and to attain wisdom. [276]

मृतस्य तु यतेर्वित्तं अश्रयेदात्मनो गुरुम् ।
गुरोर्मठं स्वशिष्यान् वा नान्यं केनापि हेतुना ॥२७७ ॥

mṛtasya tu yater vittaṁ aśrayed ātmano gurum ।
guror maṭhaṁ svaśiṣyān vā nānyaṁ kenāpi hetunā ॥277 ॥

The properties of a *saṁnyāsin*, when dead, are to be inherited by his own *guru*. Or else, it can go to the maṭha of the *guru*, or to his own disciples. No one else, in any way, has any claim on it. [277]

ज्ञानं संपादयेदस्य नित्योपासनया गुरोः ।
वेदान्ताभ्यसनेनापि मननेन च संयमी ॥२७८ ॥

jñānaṁ saṁpādayed asya nityopāsanayā guroḥ ।
vedāntābhyasanenāpi mananena ca saṁyamī ॥278 ॥

The one of self-restraint should acquire wisdom through doing services daily to one's *guru*, through repeatedly practising the tenets of Vedānta, and through contemplative self-enquiry. [278]

तावती सुखसंप्राप्तिः त्यागोऽनुष्ठीयते कियान् ।
परानन्दोपलब्ध्यर्थं त्यागं परमतो भजेत् ॥२७९ ॥

tāvatī sukhasaṁprāptiḥ tyāgo 'nuṣṭhīyate kiyān ।
parānandopalabdhyarthaṁ tyāgaṁ paramato bhajet ॥279 ॥

The extent of supreme Happiness one attains depends on the intensity of renunciation one practises. One should, therefore, in order to attain supreme Happiness, steadily observe renunciation. [279]

बिभेति यस्मान्न कश्चिदपि जीवी गतस्मयात् ।
यतेरपि भयं तस्य न कस्मादपि जीविनः ॥२८० ॥

bibheti yasmān na kaścid api jīvī gatasmayāt ।
yater api bhayaṁ tasya na kasmād api jīvinaḥ ॥280 ॥

Being not at all haughty, a *saṁnyāsin* is never feared by any living being. No living being causes fear in a *saṁnyāsin* either. [280]

मरणं जीवितं वापि नाभिनन्देद्यतिः क्वचित् ।
आज्ञामिव प्रभोर्भृत्यः कालं तु प्रतिपालयेत् ॥२८१ ॥

maraṇaṁ jīvitaṁ vāpi nābhinanded yatiḥ kvacit ।
ājñām iva prabhor bhṛtyaḥ kālaṁ tu pratipālayet ॥281 ॥

Neither death nor life is ever applauded by a *saṁnyāsin*. He simply obeys the flow of time, just as a servant does his master. [281]

संन्यासी त्यागशीलः स्याद् इति सत्यं तथाप्ययम् ।
ज्ञानार्जनं शमादींश्च शौचाचारौ न संत्यजेत् ॥२८२ ॥

saṁnyāsī tyāgaśīlaḥ syād iti satyaṁ tathāpy ayam ।
jñānārjanaṁ śamādīṁś ca śaucācārau na saṁtyajet ॥282 ॥

It is true that a *saṁnyāsin* should always be practising renunciation (*tyāga*). Still he should not renounce yearning for wisdom, the habits like self-restraint, cleanliness and customary manners. [282]

न कुप्यात् कुप्यते जातु भर्त्सयन्तं न भर्त्सयेत् ।
सस्नेहं प्रतिभाषेत प्रकामं यतिरात्मवान् ॥२८३ ॥

na kupyāt kupyate jātu bhartsayantaṁ na bhartsayet ।
sasnehaṁ pratibhāṣeta prakāmaṁ yatir ātmavān ॥283 ॥

A self-possessed *saṁnyāsin* should not become angry even with those who become angry towards him. He should not despise even those who despise him. He should talk to others lovingly with heart's content. [283]

वैदिकं ज्यौतिषं वैद्यं तर्कव्याकरणादिकम् ।
उपयुञ्जीत कृच्छ्रेऽपि नोपजीवनवर्त्मनि ॥२८४ ॥

vaidikaṁ jyautiṣaṁ vaidyaṁ tarkavyākaraṇādikam ।
upayuñjīta kṛcchre 'pi nopajīvanavartmani ॥284 ॥

A *saṁnyāsin*, even when his means of sustenance become extremely scarce, should not rely on priesthood, astrology, medicine, logical arguments and grammar for livelihood. [284]

यतिर्जीवितुमेवेह भुञ्जीत न ततोऽधिकम् ।
अतिमात्राशने रागो द्वेषो रोगश्च जायते ॥२८५ ॥

yatir jīvitum eveha bhuñjīta na tato 'dhikam ।
atimātrāśane rāgo dveṣo rogaś ca jāyate ॥285 ॥

A *yati* should eat just enough for sustaining his life, and never more than that. Eating too much arouses attachments, hatred and eventually diseases. [285]

मिताहारेण चैकान्तवासनेन्द्रियसञ्चयम् ।
नियम्योत्तमया रीत्या ध्यानयोगं च शीलयेत् ॥२८६ ॥

mitāhāreṇa caikāntavāsanendriyasañcayam ।
niyamyottamayā rītyā dhyānayogaṁ ca śīlayet ॥286 ॥

Eating moderately and living in a lonely place, a *saṁnyāsin* should practise yogic meditation properly, supported by restraint of sense-organs. [286]

सायं प्रातः स्नानपूतः प्राणायामान् विधाय षट् ।
प्रणवं निभृतं पश्चात् जपेदष्टोत्तरं शतम् ॥२८७ ॥

sāyaṁ prātaḥ snānapūtaḥ prāṇāyāmān vidhāya ṣaṭ ।
praṇavaṁ nibhṛtaṁ paścāt japed aṣṭottaraṁ śatam ॥287 ॥

Every morning and evening, after making his person clean by bathing, he should practise *prāṇāyāma* six times. This is to be followed by soundlessly repeating *praṇava* (*oṁ* or *auṁ*) one hundred and eight times. [287]

यतीनामुत्तमं धर्मं यथाशक्तिसमाहितः ।
एकान्ते सुखमासीनः समाधिमनुशील्येत् ॥२८८ ॥

yatīnām uttamaṁ dharmaṁ yathāśaktisamāhitaḥ ।
ekānte sukham āsīnaḥ samādhimanuśīlayet ॥288 ॥

By sticking to the best of the *dharma*s of *yati*s, as is one capable of, a *saṁnyāsin* should live in a lonely place, constantly practising *samādhi*. [288]

संन्यासः परमोत्कृष्टः सत्यं मानवजीविनः ।
तमासाद्य प्रमादेन नीचां वृत्तिमथाश्रयन् ॥२८९ ॥

saṁnyāsaḥ paramotkṛṣṭaḥ satyaṁ mānavajīvinaḥ ।
tamāsādya pramādena nīcāṁ vṛttim athāśrayan ॥289 ॥

अन्यापहास्यतापात्रं अधःपाताय कल्पते ।
ततो न यतिधर्मस्य विघातं जनयेद्यतिः ॥२९० ॥

anyāpahāsyatāpātraṁ adhaḥpātāya kalpate ।
tato na yatidharmasya vighātaṁ janayed yatiḥ ॥290 ॥

The most supremely laudable way of life for human beings is that of *saṁnyāsa*. For this reason, if one, after taking to it, commits error and resorts to ignoble activities, it causes his downfall, and is despised by others. A *saṁnyāsin*, therefore, should never swerve from *yati-dharma* (behaviour patterns proper to *saṁnyāsins*). [289-290]

संन्यस्तोऽप्यन्तरा कश्चिन्निर्वोढुं धर्ममक्षमः ।
यदि गेहं विशेत् पश्चात् संन्यासं नार्हति क्वचित् ॥२९१ ॥

saṁnyasto 'pyantarā kaścin nirvoḍhuṁ dharmam akṣamaḥ ।
yadi gehaṁ viśet paścāt saṁnyāsaṁ nārhati kvacit ॥291 ॥

If someone, after taking to *saṁnyāsa*, finds himself patienceless in observing the *yati-dharmas*, and enters householder's life, then he deserves no more to become a *saṁnyāsin* again. [291]

एकत्रैव मिलेत् सर्वा चातुर्मास्य उपस्थिते ।
एकस्याचार्यमुख्यस्य शिष्याणां तु परंपरा ॥२९२ ॥

ekatraiva milet sarvā cāturmāsya upasthite ।
ekasyācāryamukhyasya śiṣyāṇāṁ tu paraṁparā ॥292 ॥

All the disciples belonging to the heirarchy of a chief *guru* should gather together at one place once a year at the time of *cāturmāsya* (the four months of rainy season). [292]

यतिधर्मपराधीनः कुर्यान्न परदूषणम् ।
दूषणेनात्मनः शक्तिस्तपो बुद्धिश्च नश्यति ॥२९३ ॥

yatidharma-parādhīnaḥ kuryān na paradūṣaṇam ।
dūṣaṇenātmanaḥ śaktis tapo buddhiś ca naśyati ॥293 ॥

He who strictly observes *yati-dharmas*, should desist himself from the habit of slandering others. The habit of slandering causes damage to one's own vitality, *tapas* and proper understanding. [293]

यतिर्लोकोपकारार्थं कुर्यान्नित्यमतन्द्रितः ।
सुज्ञानाचारोपदेशमेषा साधुजनस्थितिः ॥२९४ ॥

yatir-lokopakārārthaṁ kuryān nityam atandritaḥ ।
sujñānācāropadeśam-eṣā sādhujanasthitiḥ ॥294 ॥

A *yati* (*saṁnyāsin*), for the benefit of the world, should constantly remain engaged in teaching wisdom and also customary good manners. Such is the ideal life of a *saṁnyāsin*. [294]

संन्यासी स्वस्य धर्मस्य व्रतस्याप्यपबाधकम् ।
परोपकारमखिलं कुर्वन्निष्काममास्थितः ॥२९५ ॥

saṁnyāsī svasya dharmasya vratasyāpy apabādhakam ।
paropakāram akhilaṁ kurvan niṣkāmam āsthitaḥ ॥295 ॥

A *saṁnyāsin* should live doing good to others in such a way that it does not become an obstruction to his natural way of life (*dharma*) as a renunciate. [295]